Mathematical Fundamentals of Microeconomics

C. Barry Pfitzner

Randolph-Macon College

ATOMICDOGPUBLISHING.com

Cincinnati, OH

www.atomicdog.com

ISBN 1-931442-12-6

Library of Congress Control Number: 2002100350

Printed in the United States of America by Atomic Dob Publishing, 1203 Main Street, Third Floor, Cincinnati, OH 45210.

10 9 8 7 6 5 4 3 2 1

Contents

Chapter 5

Chapter 6

Please note: we don't want you getting lost as you move between the Web and print formats, so we numbered the primary heads and subheads in each chapter the same. For example, the first primary head in Chapter 1 is labeled 1-1, the second primary head in this chapter is labeled 1-2, and so on. The subheads build from the designation of their corresponding primary head: 1-1a, 1-1b, etc.

The numbering system is designed to make moving between the online and print versions as seamless as possible. So if your instructor tells you to read the material in 2-3 and 2-4 for tomorrow's assignment, you'll know that the information appears in Chapter 2 of both the Web and print versions of the text, and you can then choose the best way for you to complete the assignment.

Preface

The idea for this book grew out of a sense of frustration from a number of years of teaching undergraduate microeconomics. That students of microeconomics at the undergraduate level can benefit from a knowledge of mathematics, especially maximization and minimization techniques, is abundantly clear; virtually every popular treatment of microeconomics includes mathematical analysis, in some cases as an integral part of the text, and in others the more advanced math is relegated to footnotes and appendices. Despite the usefulness of mathematics at this level, experience suggests that students are seldom able to grasp the mathematical analysis of microeconomics without substantial review of both algebra and calculus.

This book is intended to serve as a companion to any of the more popular texts in the field. Generally these texts make no attempt to "teach" mathematics, or simply give brief math reviews in a single chapter or appendix. It is often the case that students of microeconomics have not studied calculus at all, or may have last studied calculus as much as two years earlier. This book is intended to serve both types of students—those who have never studied calculus and those who could benefit from a review. Only an elementary knowledge of algebra on the part of the student is assumed.

Chapter 1 deals briefly with equations and graphs. This chapter should be a review for all students. Chapter 2 presents some microeconomic applications of the material from the first chapter. Chapter 3 is dedicated to differentiation and is followed by applications in Chapter 4. Chapter 5 extends the mathematics of differentiation to the important concepts of maximization and minimization, including the Lagrangian method. The final chapter, Chapter 6, applies maximization and minimization techniques to several common problems in microeconomics, including utility theory, taxation, and a duopoly model.

To make this book manageable as a companion to a main text, many topics that would be included in a more extensive treatment of mathematical economics have been left out. Prominent among these are integration methods, matrix algebra, and linear programming. Integration and matrix algebra—which are certainly essential for graduate-level microeconomics, and, perhaps, for some advanced undergraduate programs—are sacrificed here for conciseness. Linear programming, when presented in micro courses, typically includes an introduction to the topic that would make a similar introduction here redundant. In keeping with this philosophy of brevity, few proofs are offered, and methods are presented with a minimum of fanfare. If this offends the mathematical purist, he or she may consult any number of more detailed treatments of mathematical economics.

The organization and presentation of the mathematical material in this book are based on the assumption that this book is being used as a supplement in a microeconomics course. I hope that this "little book" provides a greater appreciation of the usefulness of mathematics and, in the end, enhances the student's understanding of principles of microeconomics.

Acknowledgments

A number of debts of gratitude were accumulated during the research and writing on this project. First and foremost, my friend and colleague at Randolph-Macon College, Steve Lang, read every iteration of the manuscript, offered many helpful suggestions (and corrections), and helped to write the problem sets at the end of each chapter. He also piloted sections of the text in his mathematical economics classes. I also owe thanks to another colleague, Pam Crawford of the math department, who read the manuscript and offered valuable suggestions on content and exposition.

This project was supported by a Walter Williams Craigie grant administered by Randolph-Macon College. The grant allowed me to work on the manuscript during the summer months without the distraction of other employment.

I had the good fortune to work with the fine staff at Kolb Publishing. They made the editorial and production process completely painless for me. In particular, Bob Kolb and Kateri Davis were cheerful, helpful, encouraging, and professional.

Thanks also to the Atomic Dog Publishing staff, to Vickie Putman and Nancy Sixsmith, and to freelance editor Robin Drake for their tireless efforts in converting this text to its new format.

Chapter 1

Equations and Graphs

Students of undergraduate microeconomics are already aware of the economist's affection for equations and graphs. Nearly every text in principles of economics makes liberal use of both. This chapter reviews equations and graphs that will serve as foundation material for the more advanced material in later chapters.

Outline

1-1 Variables

A *variable* is a magnitude or measurement that may vary; that is, the variable can assume different values. The price that a farmer receives for a bushel of corn is a variable, as is the grade that a student receives on an economics exam. These variables are usually denoted in mathematics by letters such as *x*, *y*, and *z*, and in economics by letters that indicate the variable being described: p for price, *mr* for marginal revenue, *tc* for total cost, and so on. Economists are also apt to confuse students with Greek letters from time to time, such as η for elasticity and perhaps π for profit. These practices should not be allowed to become bothersome; the important thing to remember is that a variable is simply a magnitude that may vary.

1-2 Equations

An *equation* is a mathematical statement indicating that two algebraic expressions are equal. The following are simple equations:

$$y = mx + b \tag{1-1}$$

$$\pi = TR - TC \tag{1-2}$$

$$P = -2Q_D + 100 \tag{1-3}$$

The student may (or may not) recognize the first equation as the general formula for a straight line. The second equation is a common way of stating that profit (π) is equal to total revenue (TR) minus total cost (TC). The third equation is, like the first, a straight line, but may also represent the relationship known as the *law of demand*, which states that price and quantity demanded vary inversely, holding other factors constant. All three equations contain the equals sign (=), without which an equation cannot be defined. In addition, an equation requires something on each side of the equals sign, even if one side is simply a number, sometimes even zero.

A variable was defined earlier as something that may change. In contrast, a *parameter* is a magnitude that is assumed to remain unchanged within the context of a particular problem. There is some tendency to use letters at the beginning of the alphabet to represent parameters and letters at the end of the alphabet to represent variables. This is a custom with many exceptions. An examination of Equation 1-1 bears this out. While y and x represent variables and b is a parameter, m is also a parameter, even though the letter *m* falls in the middle rather than at the beginning of the alphabet. The student must not expect great consistency in this regard. And because mathematical formulations in microeconomics are usually descriptive in nature, groups of letters will often be used to designate a single variable, as in Equation 1-2.

1-2a Functions

Functions represent an important class of equations. When the value of one variable depends on the value of another variable (or set of variables), these variables are said to be *functionally related*. The equation that represents the functional relationship shows *how* the variables are related. Equation 1-3 above is a function that shows how price and quantity demanded are related.

The student with a very good memory may recall that a function is a special case of a more general concept called a *relation*. A basic distinction between a relation and a function is that, for a function, each value of x (in the usual Cartesian plane) will be associated with one and only one value of y. The equation $y = 2x + 10$ is a function, since a unique value of y is determined for any specific value for x. In contrast, the equation $y = \sqrt{x}$ is a relation, because, for any positive value of x, two values of y are possible, namely, the positive and negative root values. In microeconomics, functions are utilized far more often than relations; however, both have important applications.

Much of the matter of microeconomics may be described by mathematical functions. I have already stated that price may be a function of quantity demanded. From the point of view of the buyer, it may be stated that the quantity demanded is a function of the price of the commodity. The costs of a firm are functionally related to the firm's level of output, and consumption of goods and services is functionally related to income. The use of mathematics to describe these and other economic relationships helps to simplify the concepts and enhance our understanding.

1-2b Identities

Another type of equation that is useful in economics is called an *identity*. Also called *definitional equations*, these equations are statements of equality where the left and right sides of the equation differ only in form. Equation 1-2 on page 2, which defines profit as the difference between total revenue and total cost, is an identity. It is a statement that cannot be untrue; profit must equal total revenue minus total cost regardless of the values of cost and revenue. An example of the mathematical equivalent to the identity would be an equation such as $5x = 2x + 3x$. The left side of this equation must equal the right, regardless of the value chosen for x.

In contrast, the functional equation is true only for particular values for the variables. The equation $P = -2Q_D + 100$ is true when Q_D is 20 and P is 60, but not true (the sides are unequal) if, for example, Q_D is 30 and P is 50. The difference between identity equations and functional equations is sometimes distinguished by using the "is identical to" symbol ($\equiv$) to designate identities.

1-3 Straight Lines and Their Graphs

Much of the substance of elementary economics is presented with the aid of graphs. The familiar demand and supply graphical diagram is a visual representation of two equations. For every graph in an economics textbook, there is an implied (or explicit) mathematical equation. The student will often study the graph first and the equation second, if the equation is studied at all. Economists, on the other hand, often reverse the order. Economic relationships are reduced to mathematical simplifications and then graphs are constructed from the mathematical expression. Generally, economic relationships can be reduced to mathematical expressions, which in turn can be expressed graphically.

1-3a Constant Equations

A *constant equation* exists when the value of the y variable remains fixed, regardless of the value of the x variable. The equation takes the following form:

$$y = a \qquad (1\text{-}4)$$

where a is simply some number (a parameter). For example, in the constant equation $y = 10$, y is 10 for all values of x. The graph of such an equation is a horizontal line at the value specified for y, parallel to the x axis. If $y = 8$, the graph of this function is the horizontal line shown in Figure 1-1. Such an equation could represent the demand curve for a firm operating under perfect competition, or perhaps the fixed-cost curve facing any firm in the short run. In these examples, however, the x variable would be restricted to positive values. Additionally, it is possible that the value of x is fixed for all values of y; for example, $x = 25$. In this case, the equation is not a function; rather, it is a relation, and the graph is parallel to the y axis at the value specified for x, as in Figure 1-2. This relation could be a representation of a perfectly inelastic supply or demand curve, considering only positive values of y (price).

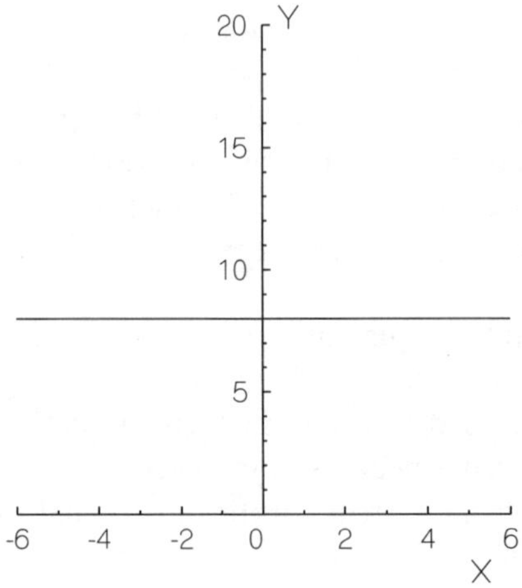

Figure 1-1
Graph of y = 8.

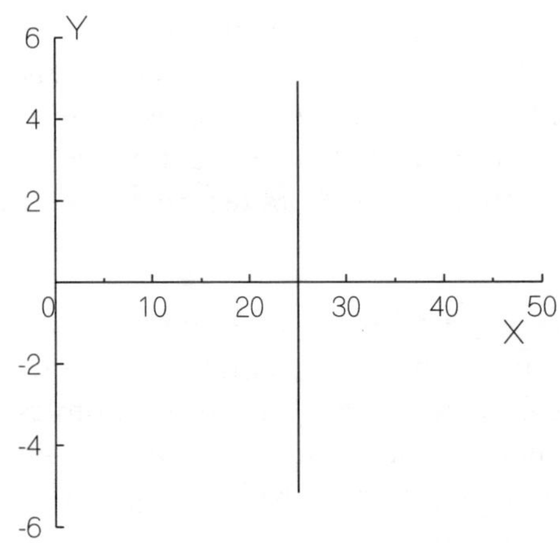

Figure 1-2
Graph of x = 25.

1-3b Linear Equations

Equations are either linear or nonlinear. A *linear equation* is a function of one variable in which the highest exponent of a variable is 1 and the variables are not multiplied by each other. Equations that do not meet these criteria are *nonlinear.* For example, the following equation is linear:

$$y = 2x + 10$$

But neither of the following is linear:

$$y = 2x^2 + 10$$

$$xy = 20$$

$y = 2x^2 + 10$ is not linear because the exponent 2 exceeds 1, and $xy = 20$ is not linear because x and y are multiplied in the equation.

A convenient form for a linear equation is called the *slope-intercept* form. That general formula, repeated from above, is as follows:

$$y = mx + b$$

The variables are y and x, and m and b are parameters. The m and the b may be positive, negative, or zero. Furthermore, when the equation is graphed in the Cartesian (xy) plane, the number b is the *y intercept.* That is, b is the value of y at which the graph crosses the y axis. The value of m is the slope of the line. (The student should remember that slope is rise over run, or $\Delta y/\Delta x$. Slope is reviewed in the following section.) Suppose that a linear equation is defined as follows:

$y = 2x - 2$

The graph of this equation should cross the y axis at –2 and have a slope of +2 (see Figure 1-3). The line crosses the y axis as promised at –2 and the slope of the line is +2, also as promised, since when x increases by 1, y increases by 2. In practice, there are a number of ways to draw linear graphs, but all methods essentially involve finding two or more points and drawing the line through those points. Notice that the graph in Figure 1-3 extends through three of the four quadrants (areas defined by the intersection of the x and y axes). That is, the line extends through quadrants where both x and y are negative or x is positive but y is negative, and the quadrant where both x and y are positive. In microeconomics, graphs are usually, although not exclusively, restricted to positive values for both x and y.

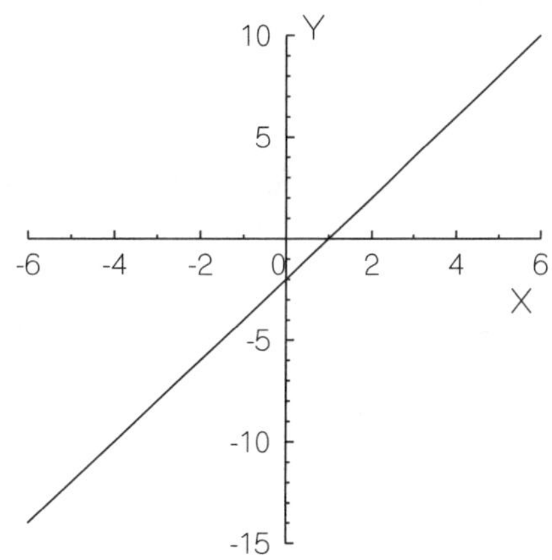

Figure 1-3
Graph of y = 2x – 2.

Suppose we want to graph another linear equation defined as follows:

$y = -5x + 20$

From the previous example, we know that the y intercept is 20; the slope of the equation in this case is –5. A simple way to graph the equation is to find "pairs" of x and y that satisfy the equation and draw a line through those pairs. For example, when x is equal to 0, y is equal to 20; this is, of course, the y intercept. When x is equal to 1, y is equal to 15. These two pairs can serve as the basis for the line to be drawn; the line simply passes through the two points defined by the pairs. Notice also that when x increased by 1 (from 0 to +1), y decreased by 5 (from 20 to 15), hence the line has a slope of –5. The graph of y = –5x + 20 is shown in Figure 1-4.

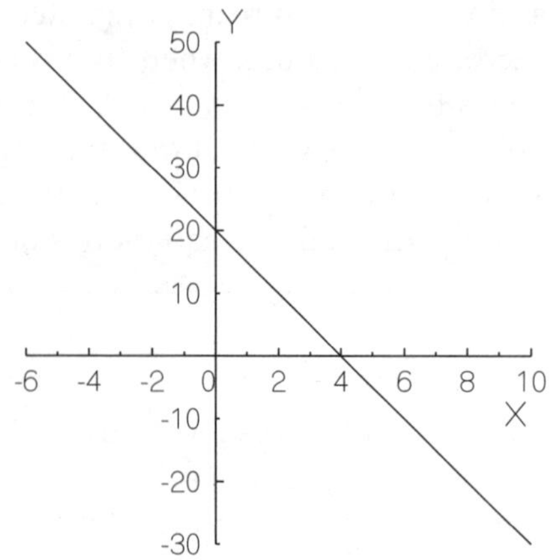

Figure 1-4
Graph of y = –5x + 20.

1-3c More on Slope

Because the slope of an equation often plays an important role in microeconomics, it deserves more extensive treatment. First, slope measures the *steepness* of any curve. It is equal to the distance moved up or down (the *rise*) divided by the distance moved right or left (the *run*). The simple mathematical formula for the slope is $\Delta y/\Delta x$, where Δ is the symbol for a small change. When the equation is linear, as are the equations whose graphs were just drawn, the slope can be found by simple inspection of the formula for the equation. The parameter attached to the x variable is the slope of that equation, and, of course, the slope of a straight line is the same at any point. When the equation is not linear, the slope is not constant, and more complex methods are needed to determine the value of the slope at different positions on the curve. The slope of a function is negative (refer to Figure 1-4) when y decreases as x increases (or y increases when x decreases) and the slope is positive (refer to Figure 1-3) when y and x move in the same direction. In either case, the line will be *steeper* the greater the absolute value of the slope. Additionally, a vertical line has infinite slope or steepness ($\Delta y/\Delta x = \infty$); a horizontal line has no steepness, and, therefore, slope of zero.

In economics, the ubiquitous marginal concept is always the slope of some "total" relationship. Marginal cost is obtained by finding the slope of the total cost function, marginal utility is the slope of the total utility function, marginal revenue is the slope of the total revenue function, and so forth. Later chapters show that finding the slope of total functions that are nonlinear and setting that slope equal to zero leads to maximum and minimum values for those functions.

1-4 Nonlinear Equations and Their Graphs

Many of the equations utilized in microeconomics are nonlinear in nature. Production functions, cost functions, and utility functions are important examples of functional relationships that often cannot be approximated well by linear equations. This section presents several types of nonlinear equations that are useful in describing microeconomic relationships.

1-4a Polynomial Functions

A *polynomial* is a type of functional form that can be used to represent a wide variety of relationships. This is the general form of a polynomial function:

$$y = a_0x^0 + a_1x^1 + a_2 x^2 + a_3x^3 + \ldots + a_nx^n$$

Of course, x^0 is by definition equal to 1, and $x^1 = x$, so the equation can also be written like this:

$$y = a_0 + a_1x + a_2x^2 + a_3x^3 + \ldots + a_nx^n \qquad (1\text{-}5)$$

The degree of a polynomial is the highest non-negative integer power of any x variable (or whatever symbol is used to represent the right-hand variable). For example, this is a first-degree polynomial:

$$y = 5 + 2x$$

And this is a fourth-degree polynomial:

$$y = 10 + 20x + 10x^2 - 2x^4$$

Notice that the first-degree polynomial is the same form as Equation 1-1, the straight line. Indeed, $y = a_0 + a_1x$ is in every way equivalent to the formula $y = mx + b$, with a_0 (instead of b) as the y intercept and a_1 (instead of m) as the slope. The straight line is therefore a special case of the general polynomial form.

If the degree of the polynomial is zero, the general equation for the polynomial (Equation 1-5) becomes $y = a_0$, where a_0 is simply some number. In fact, this is the same equation for a constant previously specified in Equation 1-4. The constant function, like the straight line, is a special case of the general polynomial form.

Two other polynomial forms are frequently encountered in microeconomics. The second-degree polynomial is also known as the *quadratic function*, and the third-degree polynomial is known as the *cubic function*. Table 1-1 summarizes the polynomial functions just described.

TABLE 1-1 Important Polynomial Functions

Functional Form	Degree	Name of Function
$y = a_0$	0	Constant function
$y = a_0 + a_1x$	1	Linear function
$y = a_0 + a_1x + a_2x^2$	2	Quadratic function
$y = a_0 + a_1x + a_2x^2 + a_3x^3$	3	Cubic function

Quadratics

The second-degree polynomial or quadratic function is often used to represent concepts in microeconomics such as demand and supply curves, cost functions, profit equations, and production functions. It is important to be able to determine the particular values of x that cause a quadratic equation to be true when a specific value for y (usually $y = 0$) is assumed. This process, which is straightforward for linear equations, is somewhat more complicated for quadratics. These values for x are called *solution values* or *critical roots.* The student should note that the quadratics presented here have two solutions; if real number solutions are required, quadratics may have only one solution value (also called *repeated roots*) or even none at all. Two methods are used to find the solution to a quadratic equation: factoring and the *quadratic formula.*

Factoring a quadratic involves starting with a product (the quadratic) and determining which two expressions (*factors*) could be multiplied to obtain that product. The method relies on the fact that if the product of two factors is equal to zero, then at least one of the two factors must also be equal to zero. Suppose we write the quadratic as $y = ax^2 + bx + c$, where a, b, and c are the parameters[1], and the quadratic can be expressed as the product of two factors of the following form:

$$(mx + n)(rx + s)$$

For y to equal zero, the first expression in parentheses must equal zero, the second expression in parentheses must equal zero, or both may equal zero.[2] By setting these factors equal to zero, the solution values can be obtained. Since this technique is one of trial and error, examples are useful for review.

Example 1

$y = x^2 + 7x + 10$ (as stated in footnote 2, factoring is easier if the x^2 term is first, followed by the x term, followed by the constant)

Find the factors $(x + ?)$ and $(x + ?)$, so that two numbers that must be found sum to 7 and when multiplied are equal to 10.

The factors are $(x + 2)$ and $(x + 5)$, and the solution values are found by setting $x + 2 = 0$ and $x + 5 = 0$. Then the solution values are $x = -2$ and $x = -5$.

Example 2

$$y = x^2 - 6x + 8$$

Find the factors $(x - ?)$ and $(x - ?)$, so that the two numbers that must be found sum to –6 and when multiplied are equal to 8.

These factors are $(x - 2)$ and $(x - 4)$, and the solution values, after setting each factor = 0, are $x = 2$ and $x = 4$.

Example 3

$$y = -2x^2 + 8x + 10$$

Find the factors $(2x + ?)$ and $(-x + ?)$, so that the two numbers to be found have a product of 10 and two times one of the numbers *minus* one times the other number equals 8.

These factors are $(2x + 2)$ and $(-x + 5)$, and the solution values are $x = -1$ and $x = 5$.

Clearly this trial-and-error process can become cumbersome and tedious for more difficult quadratics. Fortunately, the second method, the quadratic formula, solves many quadratic equations easily. The first step in using the quadratic equation is to arrange the equation (as in factoring) so that the x^2 term is first, followed by the x term, followed by the constant. Again solving the quadratic for $y = 0$, we now have the following:

$$ax^2 + bx + c \qquad (1\text{-}6)$$

1. The expression $y = ax^2 + bx + c$ is equivalent to $y = a_0 + a_1 + a_2x^2$, but the former version is more convenient for factoring and using the quadratic formula.

2. Performing the indicated multiplication of the expression $(mx + n)(rx + x)$ yields $y = ax^2 + bx + c$ as follows: $(mx)(rx) = ax^2$, the first term in the quadratic, $s(mx) + n(rx) = bx$, the second term in the quadratic, and $rs = c$, the last term.

The solution value(s), if they exist, can be calculated from the *quadratic* formula:

$$x = \frac{-b \pm \sqrt{b^2 - 4ac}}{2a} \qquad (1\text{-}7)$$

Using the values of a, b, and c from Example 3 on page 8, the solution values are found by Equation 1-7 as follows:

$$x = \frac{-8 \pm \sqrt{8^2 - 4(-2)(10)}}{2(-2)}$$

which yields the following:

$$x = \frac{-8 \pm \sqrt{144}}{-4} = \frac{-8 \pm 12}{-4}$$

and finally x = –1 and x = 5. The quadratic formula therefore offers a useful alternative to factoring when the latter is either too difficult or not obvious.

The graphs of the quadratics (often referred to as *parabolas*) also yield the same solution values that can be found by factoring or by the quadratic equation. Figure 1-5 shows the graph of Example 2 on page 8, $y = x^2 - 6x + 8$. Note that the values at which the curve crosses the x axis, +2 and +4, are x values for y = 0 (along the vertical axis) and are the same values obtained by factoring. Note also that this function reaches a minimum, or smallest value for y, where x = 3. As the student may already know (or surmise), finding these minimum points is also very important and will be a major topic for later chapters. Unlike the linear equations in section 1-3-2, "Linear Equations," the slope (steepness) of this function changes as x changes and the minimum point is evidence that the sign of the slope has changed as well. These attributes make the quadratic equation a more flexible form for representing economic relationships than the linear equation.

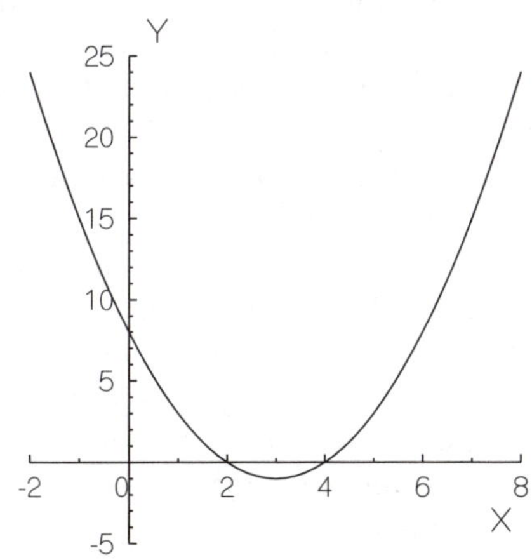

Figure 1-5
Graph of $y = x^2 - 6x + 8$.

Figure 1-6 is the graph of the quadratic function $y = -2x^2 + 8x + 10$, which is Example 3 on page 8. In this case, the function crosses the x axis at –1 and +5, the same values we found by factoring and by the quadratic formula. The slope in Figure 1-6 goes from positive values to negative values as x increases, thus reaching a maximum point. The student may guess (correctly) that in the case of these quadratics the sign attached to the x^2 term determines whether the function has a minimum point or a maximum point, or, equivalently, whether the function opens downward or upward. Additionally, in a more general discussion of parabolas, the squared term may be attached to the y variable and the relation may open to the left or to the right.

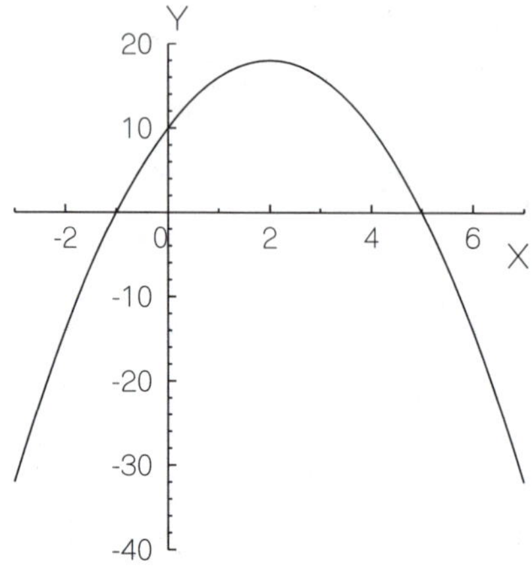

Figure 1-6
Graph of $y = -2x^2 + 8x + 10$.

Cubics

The third-degree polynomial or cubic function is so named because it includes an x^3 term. In Table 1-1, the general form of this equation is given as $y = a_0 + a_1x + a_2x^2 + a_3x^3$. The cubic function is even more flexible than the quadratic function. The addition of the last term on the right side, a_3x^3, allows the slope of the cubic function to change sign more than once. That is, the cubic may have a positive slope, then a negative slope, and then the slope may turn positive again. The slope may also change from negative to positive and back to negative as x increases.

It is also possible for the *slope* of a cubic to be either positive or negative everywhere, but alternate between increasing (becoming steeper) and decreasing (becoming flatter). The parallel to microeconomics to be gleaned here is that the cubic may be used to represent relationships that may exhibit two different *rates* of change. For example, a variable may increase at an increasing rate, then increase at a decreasing rate. Chapter 2 presents a short-run production function that behaves in this manner. Some cost functions can be expected to increase at decreasing rates followed by increasing rates.

Figures 1-7 and 1-8 demonstrate some of these properties of cubic functions. Figure 1-7 is a graph of a simple cubic function, $y = -20 + 9x + 3x^2 - x^3$. The slope of this function is negative, positive, and then negative again. The slope is zero at $x = -1$ and at $x = +3$. Notice that the function crosses the y axis at –20, the first or a_0 term in the equation. Also notice that the function crosses the x axis three times. The degree of the polynomial determines the *maximum* number of times the function may cross the x axis. The cubic crosses the x axis once or three times, and, if x is restricted to positive values, the cubic may not cross the x axis at all.

Figure 1-8 is a graph of the cubic, $y = 10x - 2x^2 + 5x^3$. This third-degree polynomial has a positive slope everywhere, but the slope declines between x values of –3 and zero and then the slope increases as x moves from zero to +3. The y intercept is zero, since the equation does not contain a constant or a_0 term, implying that $a_0 = 0$. From the previous discussion, this equation could represent an economic relationship in which some variable (y) increases as a related variable (x) increases, first at a decreasing rate and then at an increasing rate. Again, when the relationships are economic in nature, we will generally restrict both variables to positive values.

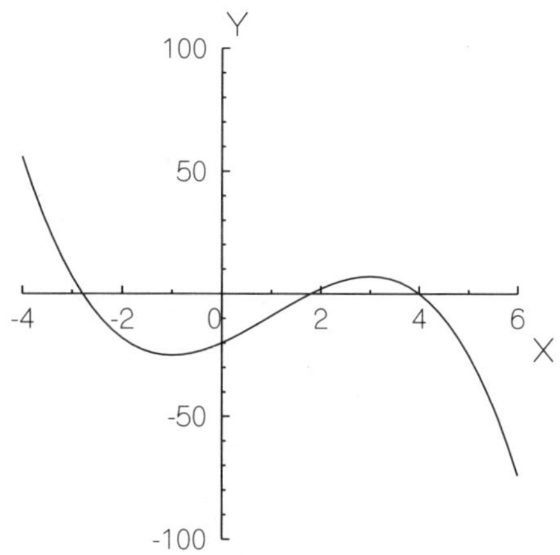

Figure 1-7
Graph of
$y = -20 + 9x + 3x^2 - x^3$.

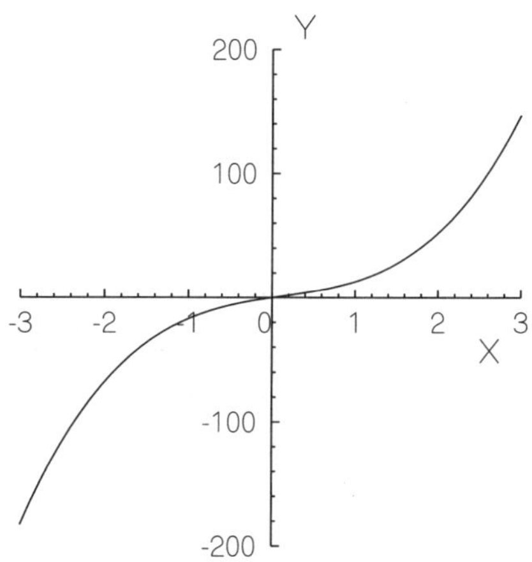

Figure 1-8
Graph of
$y = 10x - 2x^2 + 5x^3$.

1-4b Non-Polynomial Functions

A number of nonlinear functions are useful in microeconomics but do not belong to the general polynomial class defined earlier. Three nonlinear functions that are particularly valuable are the rectangular hyperbola, the exponential function, and the logarithmic function. This section presents the general form of each and the resulting graphs.

Rectangular Hyperbolas

The hyperbola can be considered a special case of a more broadly defined class of second-degree equations than that discussed earlier. The hyperbolas presented in this section are called *equilateral hyperbolas* or *rectangular hyperbolas* and are a special case of the general class of hyperbolas. The rectangular hyperbola is singled out because it is very useful for representing several important microeconomic relationships, including such commonly considered relationships as average fixed cost and demand curves with constant price elasticities. The generalized rectangular hyperbola takes this form:

$$y = c/x^n \qquad (1\text{-}8)$$

where c is a constant and n is a positive power. Also often written as $y = cx^{-n}$, this equation produces values of y that are *inversely* proportional to the positive power n of variable x. It should be clear that if the exponent n is equal to 1, then y is simply inversely proportional to the value of x or, alternatively, the product of y and x is equal to a constant, since yx = c.

Figure 1-9 is a graph of the rectangular hyperbola, y = 5/x, which may also be written yx = 5. The product of y and x must equal 5. If the product of y and x is to be a positive number, y and x must both be positive, or both must be negative. That is why there are "mirror" images in the first and third quadrants in the figure. (Quadrants are numbered one, two, three, and four, starting with the northeast and moving counter-clockwise, ending in the southeast.) Neither y nor x may be zero because y times x would then be zero. Also, the smaller the value of one of the variables, the larger the other must be—they are inversely proportional. Finally, because of the inverse proportionality, the curves move closer and closer to the y axis as x moves closer and closer to zero and, as y moves closer to zero, the curves move ever closer to the x axis. When a curve approaches an axis but never intersects the axis, it is said to be *asymptotic* to that axis or to asymptotically approach that axis. The rectangular hyperbola in Figure 1-9 is asymptotic to both axes.

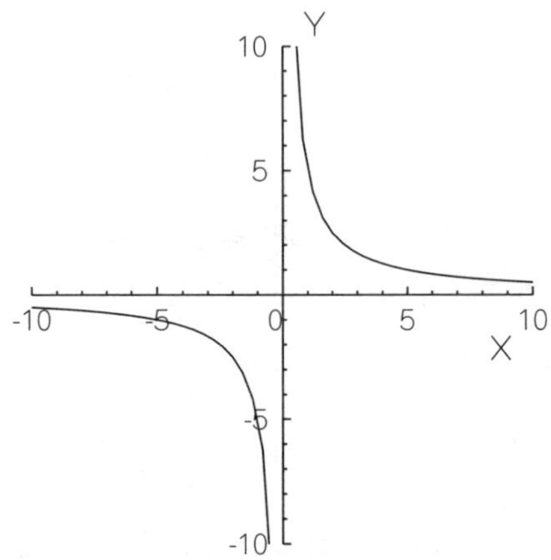

Figure 1-9
Graph of y = 5/x.

Consider the following two simple examples that can be represented by rectangular hyperbolas. Suppose that a firm has fixed costs of $5,000 (that is, fixed costs are $5,000 regardless of the level of output). If that firm were to produce 1,000 units of output, average fixed costs or AFC (fixed costs divided by output) would be $5. If output was 2,000 units, AFC would be $2.50, and so forth. This relationship would produce the curve in quadrant one of Figure 1-9, where the x axis would be output in thousands of units and the y axis would be average fixed costs in dollars. As another example, assume a child with a $5 weekly allowance spends the entire allowance on TeleTubby collecting cards. If the cards are $1 each, she buys 5 cards. When the price is 50 cents each, she buys 10 cards, etc. This demand relationship would also trace the graph in quadrant one, with price on the y axis and quantity demanded on the x axis. Note also that since price times quantity demanded always equals $5, the child has a constant price elasticity of demand equal to one, which is, by definition, unit elastic. In these examples, as I indicated would usually be the case, the negative values in the third quadrant are irrelevant from an economic point of view.

Exponential Functions[3]

Exponential functions do not appear with great frequency in typical undergraduate treatments of microeconomics. However, these functions may be used to represent many of the same relationships considered earlier in this chapter. A general formula for an exponential function is as follows:

$$y = ab^{cx} \tag{1-9}$$

where a, b, and c are (usually) positive constants, and y and x are the variables as before. The value of a is the y intercept. If the value of b is between 0 and 1 ($0 < b < +1$), the function is said to be *monotonically decreasing,* meaning that y always decreases as x increases; if $b > 1$, the function is *monotonically increasing.* (Note that b is not allowed to be less than 0, which prevents negative roots, nor is b allowed to be equal to 1, since 1 to any power is 1 and the equation would no longer be exponential.) Finally, the value of c determines how rapidly the function increases or decreases.

To illustrate some of these properties, consider the following function:

$$y = (1)3^{2x}$$

Since a = 1, the y intercept is 1 (see Figure 1-10). The function will be monotonically increasing because b is greater than 1 (b = 3). Finally, since c = 2, this function will increase twice as fast as it would if c were equal to 1, assuming that a and b have their original values.

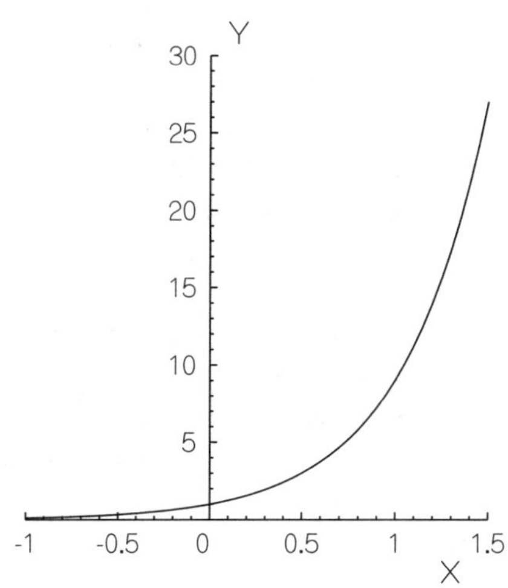

Figure 1-10
Graph of $y = (1)3^{2x}$.

The student of economics (or perhaps finance) will eventually encounter an exponential function written as follows:

$$y = Ae^{rt} \tag{1-10}$$

where A and r are positive constants as before, and e in this variation of the exponential formula is always equal to a specific constant (e = 2.71828...), the base of the natural logarithms. The superscript t has replaced the x variable and refers to

3. This section and the one that follows on logarithms may be omitted without loss in continuity.

some time period; for example, t = 5 could mean 5 years. This form of the exponential function would have the same general look as the graph in Figure 1-10, since e, which has replaced b in Equation 1-9, is greater than 1. Thus the function increases monotonically and will grow more rapidly the greater the value of r.

An important use of the $y = Ae^{rt}$ form of the exponential function is found in the area of interest compounding on financial assets. Interest is frequently compounded continuously, as opposed to quarterly, daily, or by some other frequency. Equation 1-10 computes the asset value of some principal at the end of a continuous compounding process. For example, if a principal of \$100 (A = 100) is invested at an interest rate of 10% (r = .10) for 5 years (t = 5), the value of the asset (y) at the end of 5 years is given by the following equation:

$$y = (100)(2.71828)^{(.10*5)} = 164.872 \text{ or } \$164.87$$

That is, the original \$100 will grow to \$164.87 in 5 years. This formula can be applied to other growth situations such as the sales or capital expansion path of a firm. The important feature of this form is that the value of r derived by simple inspection of the expression will always represent the *instantaneous* rate of growth of the base A.

Logarithms and Logarithmic Functions

The *logarithm* (often abbreviated *log*) of a number is an exponent to which the base must be raised to produce that number. Students will likely remember that the base of the *common* logarithms is the number 10. If we wanted to find the common logarithm of the number 100, the answer would be 2, since $10^2 = 100$. The log of 10,000 would be 4, since $10^4 = 10{,}000$. In each case, the base is the number 10, and 2 and 4 are the exponents to which 10 must be raised to produce the numbers 100 and 10,000, respectively. Therefore we can write log 100 = 2 and log 10,000 = 4. If the number for which we want to find the common logarithm is between 0 and 1, the logarithm is negative. For example, the logarithm of .01 is –2, since $1/10^2 = 10^{-2} = .01$; thus 10 must be raised to the –2 power to yield the number .01.

In theoretical work, the preferred logarithmic base is the number e, where e again is a constant approximately equal to 2.71828. These logarithms are called *natural logs* or *Naperian logs* after their discoverer, John Napier (1550–1617). The conventions for distinguishing natural logs from common logs are uncomplicated. Log and $\log_{10}$ refer to common logarithms, and $\log_e$ or simply ln (which seems to be the preferred notation at present) represents natural logarithms. Used in conjunction with exponential functions in which e is raised to some exponent (say n), natural logs require no computation. In general, $\ln e^n = n$. As examples, consider the following:

$$\ln e^2 = 2$$

$$\ln e^5 = 5$$

$$\ln e^{.75} = .75$$

$$\ln 1 = \ln e^0 = 0 \text{ (remember, any number to the power 0 is 1)}$$

$$\ln 1/e = \ln e^{-1} = -1$$

Several other rules of logarithms are important to remember. These rules are summarized in the appendix to this chapter.

A quick and simple example of the usefulness of logarithms can be advanced by considering the Cobb-Douglas production function. This formulation, which is introduced in nearly every treatment of microeconomics at the undergraduate level, is given by Equation 1-11:

$$Q = AK^{\alpha}L^{\beta} \tag{1-11}$$

where Q = output, K = capital input, L = labor input, and A, α, and β are all positive constants. Although this equation in not linear in the variables, following the rules of logarithms from the appendix, it is linear in the coefficients of the logarithms:

$$lnQ = lnA + \alpha\, lnK + \beta lnL$$

This form of the equation is easy to estimate using econometric methods (once we have the data), and the values of α and β are the elasticities of output with respect to capital input and labor input, in that order. That is, the value of, say, α represents the percentage change in output that would result from a 1% change in the level of capital input. This important form of the production function and its rich implications are examined more closely in subsequent chapters.

Logarithmic functions will be monotonically (or strictly) decreasing if the base is between 0 and 1, and monotonically increasing if the base is greater than 1. Since the most useful logarithmic bases are greater than 1, we will deal with only the graphs of monotonically increasing functions.

Logarithmic Functions and Exponential Functions as Inverses

We have already seen that a close relationship exists between logarithmic functions and exponential functions: Logarithms are exponents, the base of the natural logarithms is a preferred base for exponential functions, logarithmic transformations reduce exponential functions to linear forms, etc. In fact, the two types of functions are what is known as inverse functions of each other. It is enough to know at this point that an *inverse* function will produce a "mirror image" graph of its corresponding function. This means that if we interchanged the axes in an exponential graph, we would have the graph of its logarithmic inverse. The exponential function $y = e^x$ has a corresponding inverse function $y = \ln(x)$. These inverses of exponential functions are easily found as follows: Using logs of the exponential function, reverse the positions of x and y in the result, which is equivalent to interchanging the axes. In the case of $y = e^x$, the transformation would be as follows:

$$ln(y) = x\, ln(e) = x \text{ (since } ln(e) = 1)$$

Reversing the positions of x and y, we have this:

$$y = ln(x)$$

Figure 1-10 graphed the exponential function $y = (1)3^{2x}$. The corresponding log function can be found by again taking logs:

$$ln(y) = ln(1) + 2x\, ln(3), \text{ solving for x}$$

$$x = ln(y)/(2\, ln(3)), \text{ since } ln(1) = 0$$

and interchanging x and y:

$y = ln(x)/(2\ ln(3))$

This result, $y = \ln(x)/(2 \ln(3))$, is graphed along with its inverse function $y = (1)3^{2x}$ in Figure 1-11. The exponential function has the y intercept of 1 as before, whereas the log function has an x intercept of 1. The exponential function increases at an increasing rate; the logarithmic function increases at a decreasing rate. Finally, the two functions are symmetric about a 45-degree line through the origin.

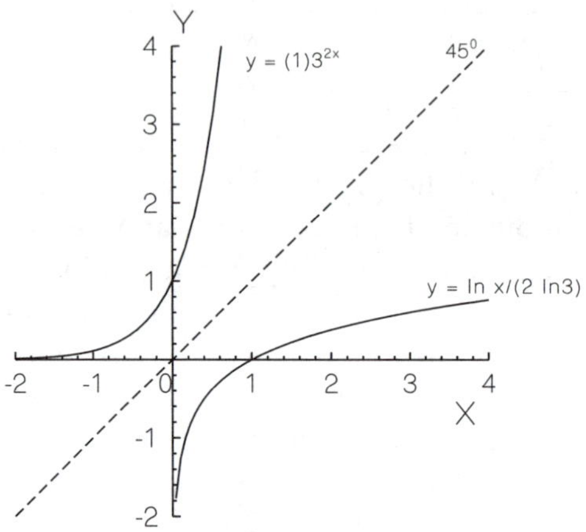

Figure 1-11
Graph of $y = (1)3^{2x}$ and its inverse $y = \ln x/(2 \ln 3)$.

Logarithms are important and powerful tools in mathematics. They are also indispensable for estimating many economic relationships both at the macro and micro levels. However, their treatment in microeconomics at the undergraduate level is usually limited to such simple tasks as reducing multiplicative relationships to linear ones, as in the Cobb-Douglas production function. In keeping with the philosophy of this chapter, this section is intended to present only material necessary to understanding those uses of logs that the student is likely to encounter in the micro course.

1-5 Functions of More Than One Variable

It is often necessary to specify equations in which a variable depends on more than a single other variable. Even armed with the economist's ability to make simplifying assumptions, in many cases it is more realistic and still manageable to approximate economic relationships wherein a variable depends on two or more variables. In the preceding section, a production function was presented in which output is a function of two variables: the stock of capital and the labor force. Utility functions are another prominent application in which a single variable, utility, is usually depicted as a function of two (or more) goods. Many other relationships, such as demand, are often simplified to functions of a single variable only by using the "ceteris paribus" assumption; that is, holding other influences constant. In the case of demand, this requires holding other prices, income, tastes and preferences, and the like constant in order to isolate the effect of the price of a good on its quantity demanded. The student will encounter still other examples of functions of more than one variable in the study of microeconomics.

These functions of more than one variable are as varied in mathematical form as are functions of single variables. Indeed, since a function of multiple variables may contain any number of the forms presented earlier (and still others), it is safe to say that the possibilities are unlimited. Fortunately, at the undergraduate level in microeconomics, a relatively small number of functional forms appear.

It is often difficult to interpret graphs of functions of two variables, and graphs of functions of more than two variables would be unintelligible to all of us. Figure 1-12 is an example of what a graph of a Cobb-Douglas production function looks like with Q, K, and L axes representing output, capital stock, and labor, respectively. The specific form of this function is $Q = 5K^{.4}L^{.6}$. The interpretation of the graph is relatively straightforward. The student should observe that, if both capital and labor are increased, the level of the surface, which is output, also increases. In addition, if, say, labor is held at some specific level and capital is increased, the level of output rises. In fact, if a specific value for labor is chosen, such as L = 2, and a *contour* line is followed as capital (K) is increased, it is possible to observe that output increases more slowly as equal amounts of capital are added. This is the famous *diminishing marginal returns* concept that is central to production theory. The Cobb-Douglas production function exhibits this and many other "nice" properties discussed in later chapters.

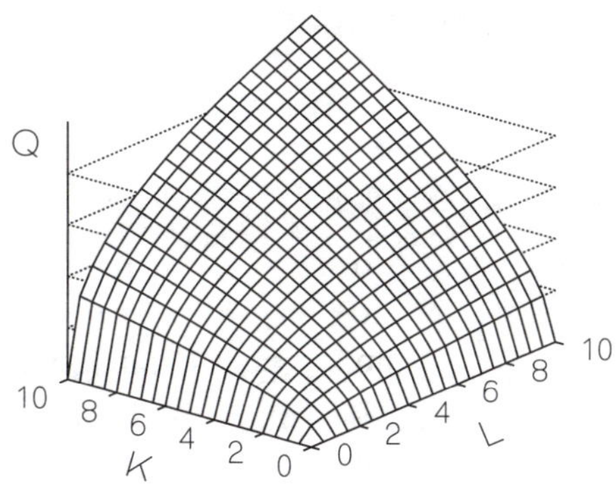

Figure 1-12
Graph of $Q = 5K^{.4}L^{.6}$.

1-6 Summary

This chapter began by introducing a number of definitions necessary for considering equations and graphs. Next, various linear equations and their graphs were reviewed and the concept of slope discussed. Nonlinear equations were presented and divided into polynomials and non-polynomials. Finally, there was a short introduction to functions of more than one variable.

The overriding idea of this chapter is to get the student "up to speed"; that is, to review only those types of equations that are likely to be encountered in undergraduate microeconomics. Much, therefore, has been left out. Trigonometric functions, for example, are not considered at all, and other concepts are given brief treatment. This is by design. The purpose here is not to present a full mathematical treatise, but rather to help the student more fully understand the concepts of microeconomics.

Appendix

Rules for Exponents

There are a number of useful rules for exponents that should be familiar. Table 1-2 shows each rule and an example.

TABLE **1-2** **Rules for Exponents**

Rule 1: $x^m x^n = x^{m+n}$	Example: $x^2 x^3 = x^5$
Rule 2: $x^m/x^n = x^{m-n}$	Example: $x^6/x^2 = x^{6-2} = x^4$
Rule 3: $x^{-n} = 1/x^n$	Example: $x^{-3} = 1/x^3$
Rule 4: $x^0 = 1$	Example: $5^0 = 1$
Rule 5: $x^{1/n} = \sqrt[n]{x}$	Example: $x^{1/3} = \sqrt[3]{x}$
Rule 6: $(x^m)^n = x^{mn}$	Example: $(x^2)^3 = x^6$
Rule 7: $x^n y^n = (xy)^n$	Example: $x^3 y^3 = (xy)^3$

Rules for Logarithms

Table 1-3 shows some useful rules and examples for logarithms. The rules are stated for natural logs but, with the exception of the first rule, they apply to common logs as well. Also recall that logs do not exist for negative numbers or 0.

TABLE **1-3** **Rules for Logarithms**

Rule 1: $\ln e^x = x$	Example: $\ln e^5 = 5$
Rule 2: $\ln(xy) = \ln x + \ln y$	Example: $\ln(e^3 e2) = \ln e^3 + \ln e^2 = 3 + 2 = 5$
Rule 3: $\ln(x/y) = \ln x - \ln y$	Example: $\ln(10/5) = \ln 10 - \ln 5$
Rule 4: $\ln x^n = n \ln x$	Example: $\ln x^4 = 4 \ln x$

These rules are often used as simplifying devices in problems of calculation and statistical estimation. Recognize that the rules can be used in combination.

Example:

$$w = (x^4 y^6 / z^2)e^3$$

$$\ln w = \ln(x^4 y^6) - 2 \ln z + 3$$

$$= 4 \ln x + 6 \ln y - 2 \ln z + 3$$

Problems

1. Sketch the graphs of the following linear equations.
   (a) $y = 50$
   (b) $x = 10$
   (c) $y = 24 - 4x$
   (d) $y = 200 + .5x$
   (e) $Q_d = 100 - 5P$
   (f) $y = -10 + 2x$

2. Determine the slope of each of the equations in problem 1.

3. Solve the following quadratics (set $y = 0$) by factoring or by the quadratic formula.

   (a) $y = x^2 + x - 12$
   (b) $y = x^2 - 7x + 10$
   (c) $y = -2x^2 + 3x + 20$
   (d) $y = 16x^2 - 5x - 30$

4. Identify the following as constant equations, straight lines, quadratic equations, cubic equations, hyperbolas, or exponential equations.

   (a) $y = 50$
   (b) $P = \$100$
   (c) $y = 7x - 20$
   (d) $Q_d = 100 - 5P$
   (e) $y = x^2 + 3x + 5$
   (f) $y = 5x^3$
   (g) $y = x^3 - 2x^2 + 10$
   (h) $y = 250/x^2$
   (i) $y = 10x^{-1}$
   (j) $y = 200e^{.10t}$
   (k) $y = (4)5^{2x}$

5. Sketch the graphs of the following nonlinear equations.

   (a) $y = x^2 - 10x + 20$
   (b) $y = -3x^2 + 36x + 10$
   (c) $y = x^3/10 - 5x^2 + 100x$
   (d) $y = 50/x$
   (e) $y = (10)3^{2x}$
   (f) $y = 2 \log(2x)$

Chapter 2

Microeconomic Applications of Equations and Graphs

This chapter presents a number of applications of the mathematical tools that were reviewed in Chapter 1, "Equations and Graphs." The examples are chosen to coincide with those that the student is likely to encounter in his or her microeconomics course.

Outline

2-1 Linear Demand and Supply Curves

Chapter 1 introduced the linear equation $y = mx + b$, pointing out that when linear equations describe economic relationships, the y and x variables are commonly replaced with letters representing economic variables. Thus, Equation 2-1 is a linear equation that represents a demand function:

$$P = 100 - 2Q_d \tag{2-1}$$

Here, P is the price per unit and Q_d is the quantity demanded for some unit of time. The vertical intercept, along the P axis, is 100, and the slope is –2. As mentioned in Chapter 1, the order of the terms of the equation is unimportant. The equation could be "solved" for Q_d without changing the meaning of the function:

$$Q_d = 50 - .5P$$

This is a simple rearrangement of Equation 2-1. Many economists would prefer the second version of the equation for the subtle reason that, at least from the buyer's viewpoint, quantity demanded is a function of price. Price is the "cause" and quantity demanded is the "effect." Tradition, on the other hand, dictates that the graphical form of the demand curve should have price on the vertical axis and quantity demanded on the horizontal axis. Because most demand (and supply) equations can be rearranged without great effort, the different forms of the equations should not be an annoyance.

Suppose we write an equation for supply to go with our demand equation above:

$$P = 3Q_S \tag{2-2}$$

When solved for Q_S, the supply equation can be written as $Q_S = P/3$. Assuming that these equations are market demand and supply curves for some product, say gasoline in some bygone era, where P is price in cents and Q is millions of gallons of gasoline per month, we should be able to solve the equations *simultaneously* for the competitive equilibrium. This process is known as solving a *system* of equations. Because we already know that a competitive equilibrium means a single price and quantity demanded equals quantity supplied ($Q_d = Q_S = Q$), we can replace the Q_d and the Q_S with Q, leaving two equations in two unknowns:

$$P = 100 - 2Q$$
$$P = 3Q$$

One way to solve these equations is to eliminate one of the two variables, leaving one equation in one unknown. We could eliminate either the P or the Q from each equation, but the P will be easier because the equations are already stated explicitly in terms of P. Since $P = 100 - 2Q$, and $P = 3Q$, it follows that

$$100 - 2Q = 3Q$$

Adding 2Q to both sides of the equation gives us the result:

$$100 = 5Q$$

and dividing both sides by 5 yields

$$Q = 20$$

or 20 million gallons per month.

To find the equilibrium price, simply substitute Q = 20 into either of the original equations. Choosing the supply function,

$$P = 3(20) = 60$$

or 60¢ per gallon. This competitive market is in equilibrium with a price of 60¢ per gallon and 20 million gallons sold per month.

Although empirical research would seldom find demand and supply curves that are linear, these equations often are close approximations to their "real world" cousins and yield the same principal results. It is for these reasons and simplicity of exposition that linear demand and supply are used so frequently in economics texts.

2-1a Excise Taxes

An excise tax levied on goods or services in a competitive market is analyzed easily in the context of linear demand and supply curves. Suppose, in the example in the preceding section, the government decides to levy a 25¢ per gallon tax on the sellers of gasoline. The effect of this tax is to shift the supply curve *vertically upward* by the amount of the tax (with P on the vertical axis; see Figure 2-1, a little later in this section). In terms of the supply equation, $P = 3Q_S$, this shift is accomplished by simply adding 25 to the right side of the equation (or, equivalently, subtracting 25 from the left side) resulting in this "new" supply curve:

$$P = 25 + 3Q_S \qquad (2\text{-}3)$$

Why is this the effect on the supply curve? The original supply curve shows the various amounts of gasoline that suppliers are willing to supply at alternative prices prior to taxation. Because for each gallon sold after the tax is imposed, sellers must pay 25¢ to the government, sellers will now require 25¢ more per gallon than before for each possible quantity supplied. Note that the economic behavior of the sellers regarding what might be called the "net" price has not changed. If sellers sold, say, 16 million gallons of gasoline before the tax, the supply price would be 48¢ per gallon (P = 3(16) = 48). With the "new" supply curve, the supply price for those same 16 million gallons would be 73¢ per gallon (P = 25 + 3(16) = 73). The sellers would receive 73¢ for each gallon, pay the government 25¢ for each, and be left with the same "net" price of 48¢ (73¢ – 25¢). The same analysis would follow for any other quantity along the supply curve, thus producing a supply curve that has shifted vertically upward by the amount of the tax.[1]

It is now possible to calculate the equilibrium price and quantity as before based on the original demand curve, which is unaffected by this tax, and the "new" supply curve. The equations to be solved are

1. Note that the vertical shift in the supply curve is a decrease in supply, since an upward vertical shift is also a leftward shift (refer to Figure 2-1).

$$P = 100 - 2Q_d$$

$$P = 25 + 3Q_S$$

Equilibrium requires $Q_d = Q_S$, so the subscripts may be dropped from the Q's. Also, because there is a single price, P, we may write the equation as follows:

$$100 - 2Q = 25 + 3Q$$

and

$$75 = 5Q$$

$$Q = 15$$

The equilibrium quantity is 15 million gallons per month, 5 million fewer than before the tax.

Now to find the equilibrium price and the division of the tax. The equilibrium price after the tax can be found by substituting the equilibrium quantity into either the demand equation (Equation 2-1), or the "new" supply equation (Equation 2-3). Choosing the latter, we get the result:

$$P = 25 + 3(15) = 70$$

or 70¢ per gallon.

Notice that the 70¢ per gallon is only 10¢ higher than the 60¢ price prior to the tax. The buyer pays 10¢ more per gallon. We know, however, that the tax is 25¢ on each gallon sold. Where, then, is the rest of the 25¢? The answer is that the seller who receives a market price of 70¢ must pay the 25¢ to the government leaving a "net" price of 45¢, or 15¢ less than the original 60¢. In this case, the major portion of the tax is borne by the seller.

Figure 2-1 is a graphical representation of the effects of the 25¢ excise tax. The initial demand and supply curves intersect at E_1, with equilibrium price of 60¢ per gallon and equilibrium quantity of 20 million gallons. The excise tax shifts the supply curve vertically by the amount of the tax to the "S + tax" line in the graph, producing the new equilibrium at E_2, with market price now 70¢ per gallon, and equilibrium quantity of 15 million gallons. The buyer again pays 10¢ per gallon more than before the tax. The seller collects a market price that is 10¢ higher than before, but must pay the 25¢ tax to the government, leaving a net price that is 15¢ lower for each gallon than before the tax.

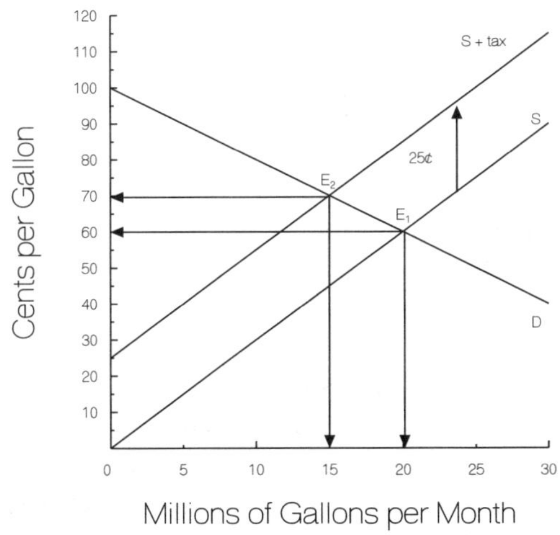

Figure 2-1
Excise tax on seller.

The way the tax is ultimately divided between the buyer and seller is determined by the sensitivity of demand and supply to changes in price. Given the demand curve, the seller will bear a larger share of the tax (and the buyer a smaller share) when the quantity supplied is less sensitive[2] to price changes. With a given supply curve, the buyer will bear a larger share of the tax (and the seller a smaller share) when the quantity demanded is less sensitive to price changes.

Taxes are not always collected from sellers. Suppose that instead of the 25¢ excise tax on the sellers, buyers were required to buy a 25¢ coupon from the government for each gallon purchased. How would the original demand and supply curves be affected? What would be the new equilibrium price and quantity? And how would the tax be divided between the sellers and buyers? To start, the demand curve would shift *vertically downward* by the amount of the tax. The reasoning for the downward shift of the demand curve is similar to the reasoning for the upward shift of the supply curve when the tax is to be remitted by the seller. The buyer now must pay a "total" price that includes the market price of the gallon plus the 25¢ tax, in the form of a coupon, to the government. Buyers are now willing to pay 25¢ less for any given quantity of gallons than before the imposition of the tax. A convenient way to write this new demand curve is simply to add 25¢ to the left side of the demand equation, denoting the fact that the total price paid by the buyer is the market price plus the tax:

$$P + 25 = 100 - 2Q_d$$

and rearranging,

$$P = 75 - 2Q_d \tag{2-4}$$

Now, solving the original supply curve (Equation 2-2) and the "new" demand curve (Equation 2-4) simultaneously, equilibrium values will be found for price and quantity, and ultimate division of the tax can be ascertained. Dropping the subscripts on the Q's (since $Q_d = Q_S$) and noting that $P = 75 - 2Q_d$ and $P = 3Q_S$, we can write the following:

2. At this point, many texts will say less elastic rather than less sensitive (steeper, graphically). Even though we must be careful not to confuse elasticity and slope, it is nonetheless true that for a given price and quantity combination, a steeper curve is a less elastic curve.

$$75 - 2Q = 3Q$$
$$75 = 5Q$$
$$15 = Q$$

The equilibrium quantity is 15, just as it was when the tax was nominally on the seller. What of the division of the burden of the tax? First we need to find the market price by substituting the quantity into either the demand or the supply equation. Choosing the demand equation this time, $P = 75 - 2(15)$ or $P = 45¢$. Now the seller receives 15¢ less per gallon (60¢ – 45¢) than before any tax was imposed. The buyer pays a market price of 45¢ plus the coupon fee of 25¢, for a total price of 70¢, 10¢ more than the original price. Again, the buyer ultimately bears 10¢ of the tax and the other 15¢ of the tax falls on the seller, just as was the case with the excise tax. Figure 2-2 shows the downward shift in the demand curve by the amount of the tax (coupon fee), with the new market equilibrium price of 45¢.

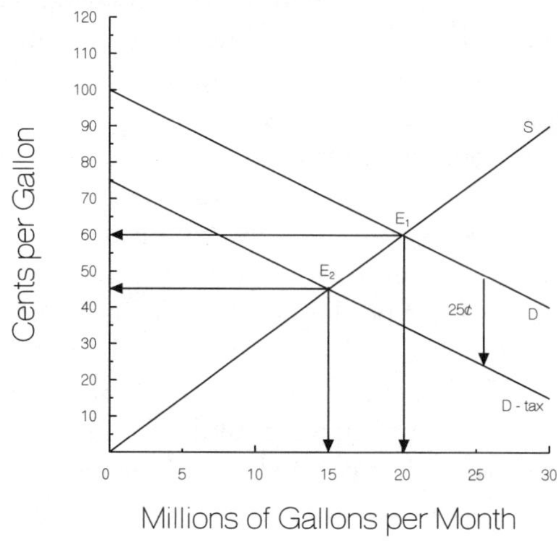

Figure 2-2
Tax on the buyer.

The moral to be gleaned here is that the legal incidence of the tax is of no consequence in determining the ultimate burden of the tax. What matters is the sensitivity of the demand and supply curves to changes in price.

As a final note on finding a demand or supply equation after the imposition of a tax, consider the case where the equation is written with Q as a function of price, for example, $Q_S = (1/3)P$. The equation could, of course, be rewritten with P on the left side. However, it is simpler to recognize that in the case of a 25¢ excise tax, the seller receives what we have called a "net" price that is 25¢ less than the market price. That is, the net price is $P - 25$, and it is the net price that matters to the seller. Hence, we can write this:

$$Q_S = (1/3)(P - 25)$$
$$Q_S = (1/3)P - 8\ 1/3$$

which is simply another form of $P = 25 + 3Q_S$. The same solution values would result with either form.

2-1b Price Elasticity and Straight-Line Demand Curves

Nearly every treatment of price elasticity of demand will eventually present the following formula:[3]

$$\eta_d = \frac{-\Delta Q}{Q} \div \frac{\Delta P}{P} \qquad (2\text{-}5)$$

where η_d is price elasticity of demand, the numerator on the right side of the expression represents the percentage change in quantity demanded, and the denominator represents the percentage change in price. This formula is appropriate for measuring price elasticity at a single point on a demand curve, or between points that are very close to each other. To demonstrate, rearrange the elasticity formula (multiply the numerator and denominator by $P/\Delta P$ and exchange the positions ΔP and Q in the denominator) to obtain the result:

$$\eta_d = \frac{-\Delta Q}{\Delta P} \cdot \frac{P}{Q} \qquad (2\text{-}6)$$

The first ratio in the product to the right of the equals sign, $-\Delta Q/\Delta P$, is -1 times the inverse of the slope of a demand curve, where P is on the vertical axis and Q on the horizontal axis. We know that the slope of any straight line is a constant and, therefore, so is the inverse of the slope. Then the elasticity coefficient will change each time the P, Q combination changes. Again, consider the demand equation for gasoline:

$$P = 100 - 2Q_d$$

Suppose we want to find the price elasticity for the point on the demand curve where $P = 80$ and $Q_d = 10$. By inspecting the formula, we can determine that the slope of the demand equation, $\Delta P/\Delta Q_d$, is -2; therefore, $-\Delta Q_d/\Delta P$ is $1/2$. Since $P/Q_d = 8$ at this point on the demand curve, $\eta_d = (1/2)(8) = 4$. For a different P, Q combination, say, $P = 40$ and $Q_d = 30$, the price elasticity would be different, $\eta_d = (1/2)(4/3) = 2/3$ or .67.

A closer look at the graph of the demand equation will further clarify some of these ideas. The demand curve and the two elasticity coefficients just computed are reproduced in Figure 2-3. Notice that the higher value is nearer the upper end of the line and the smaller value is toward the lower end of the curve. This is a general result for straight-line demand curves that slope downward and to the right. Extending this notion, as we approach the vertical axis along the demand line, the elasticity coefficient approaches infinity; and as we approach the horizontal axis, the coefficient approaches zero. It is furthermore true that the coefficient is equal to 1 at the midpoint on the demand line. These latter properties should not be surprising; using Equation 2-6, the coefficient of elasticity is computed as follows:

$$\eta_d = (\tfrac{1}{2}) \cdot (P/Q)$$

3. The negative sign in Equation 2-4 makes the coefficient positive (because the demand curve is negatively sloped). Some authors choose not to include the negative sign; if this is the case, the coefficient is negative.

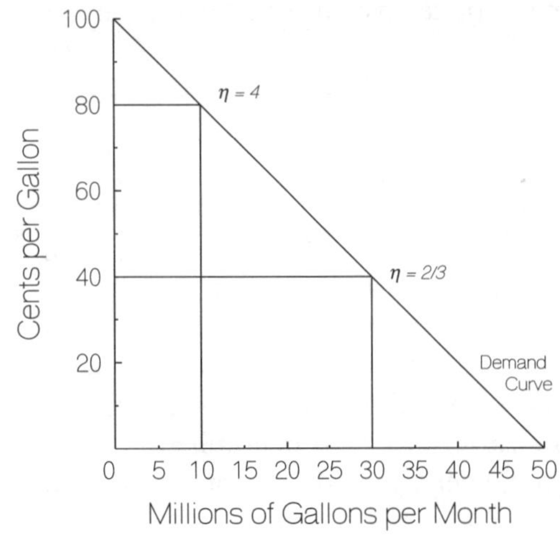

Figure 2-3
Straight-line demand elasticity.

Thus, as P/Q becomes larger approaching the vertical axis, the value of the elasticity coefficient becomes larger. And since P/Q becomes smaller as we approach the horizontal axis, the value of the coefficient also becomes smaller.

Consider a generic demand curve of the form P = a – bQ, graphed in Figure 2-4. The letter *z* represents some arbitrary point on the demand curve. We can now show that the elasticity at point z is equal to the ratio of line segments zc and az; that is, zc/az.

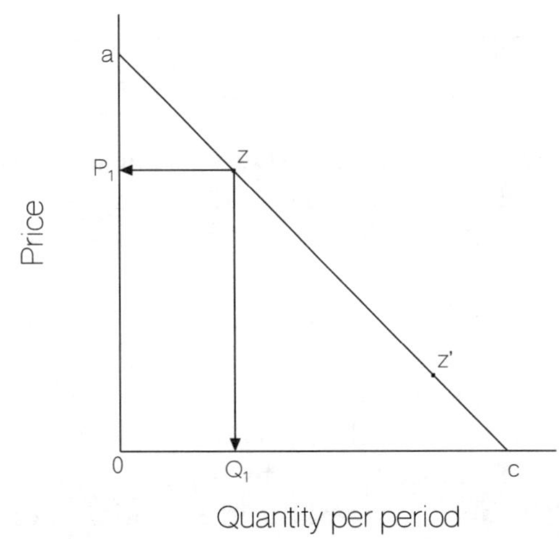

Figure 2-4
Generalized straight-line demand elasticity.

Referring again to the elasticity formula in Equation 2-6, –ΔQ/ΔP is –1 times the inverse of the slope of the demand curve. Since the demand curve is a straight line, the slope can be measured between any two points on the line. Suppose we choose to measure the slope between points a and z. As we move along the curve from a to z, price would fall by the "amount" aP_1 and quantity would increase by the amount $0Q_1$, or slope is equal to $-aP_1/0Q_1$. To get –ΔQ/ΔP, simply invert $-aP_1/0Q_1$ and multiply by –1, which gives us $0Q_1/aP_1$. Since elasticity is to be evaluated at point z, the price is $0P_1$ and the quantity is $0Q_1$. The expression for elasticity is now as follows:

$$\eta_d = \frac{0Q_1}{aP_1} \bullet \frac{0P_1}{0Q_1}$$

Then, by canceling,

$$\eta_d = \frac{0P_1}{aP_1}$$

And since the distance $0P_1$ is equal to the distance zQ_1,

$$\eta_d = \frac{zQ_1}{aP_1}$$

The triangle bounded by azP_1 is *similar* to the triangle bounded by zcQ_1 and the ratios of corresponding legs of similar triangles are equal. Then it follows that

$$\eta_d = \frac{zQ_1}{aP_1} = \frac{Q_1c}{P_1z} = \frac{zc}{az} \qquad (2\text{-}7)$$

Clearly, if point z is above the midpoint of the demand line, the line segment zc is larger than line segment az, and the elasticity coefficient is greater than 1. If the point at which we want to evaluate elasticity is below the midpoint, say z′, the elasticity coefficient is less than 1, since line segment z′c would be less than line segment az′. Only at the midpoint of the demand curve is $\eta_d = 1$. It should be emphasized that not all demand curves have all ranges of elasticity. As indicated in Chapter 1, and as we will see in Chapter 4, it is possible to write expressions for demand curves with *constant* elasticities.

As a final observation for this section, note that the methodology derived above can be applied to nonlinear curves. Simply draw a tangent to the curve where elasticity is to be evaluated and use the tangent line to find *any* of the line segment ratios in Equation 2-7.

2-2 A Short-Run Production Function

A common application of cubic functions (third-degree polynomials) is the production function in the short run. In the short run, at least one factor of production is fixed, and usually it is assumed that production is then determined by only one variable factor. Suppose that production in the short run is determined by the quantity of labor hired. Let TP stand for total product and L stand for the quantity of labor measured in hundreds of "person" hours. Mathematically, then, total product is a function of labor only. Let the exact form of the function be as follows:

$$TP = 12L^2 - L^3 \qquad (2\text{-}8)$$

Several characteristics of Equation 2-8 are easily observed. First, it does not contain a constant term; therefore, the function will intersect the origin. Second, the first term on the right side, $12L^2$, is positive—by itself this term would cause the TP value to increase at an increasing rate (only positive values for L are sensible). Third, however, the L^3 term ($-1L^3$) is negative. Under these conditions, the function will first increase at an increasing rate, then at a decreasing rate, and eventually TP will fall and even become negative. The falling and negative sections of TP are not relevant to economics, as no firm would hire labor or any other factor that would cause output to fall.

Equation 2-8 is graphed in Figure 2-5. Notice that TP increases at an increasing rate up to four (hundred) person hours; that is, the function is concave from above between the origin and 4. In this region, each time labor input increases by one unit, total product increases by a larger amount than it did with the preceding unit increase of labor. Between four and eight units of labor, each time the number of labor units increases by one, total product increases by a smaller (positive) amount. Stated differently, the slope of the TP schedule is increasing between zero and four units of labor and decreasing between four and eight. This point on the function where concavity changes is known as an *inflection point*, and it lies directly above 4 on the horizontal axis. After eight units of labor, the slope is negative, indicating that total product is decreasing.[4]

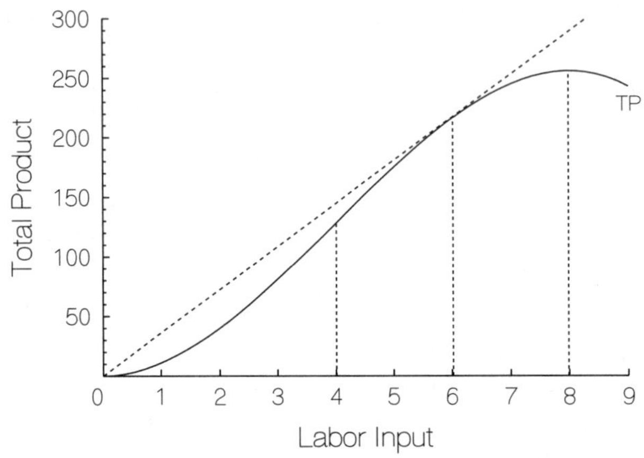

Figure 2-5
A short-run production function.

We can immediately derive the average product curve from the total product curve in Equation 2-8. Because average product is defined as the ratio of total product to the number of units of the variable factor (labor in this case), we need only to divide each term in Equation 2-8 by L, which yields the following:

$$AP_L = TP/L = 12L - L^2 \qquad (2\text{-}9)$$

where AP_L indicates the average product of labor. This average product function is graphed in Figure 2-6. Notice that the average product reaches a maximum at six units of labor. The maximum of average product may also be found from the original production function by drawing a straight line through the origin that is tangent to the production function.[5] Such a line is drawn in Figure 2-5. The tangency position is above six units of labor input, the same number of units directly under the maximum level of average product that can be found by inspecting Figure 2-6.

The positions of maximum of total product, maximum of average product, and points of inflection play important roles in the economics of short-run production and cost. Beginning with Chapter 3, I will introduce very simple methods for finding these same positions based on the use of calculus.

4. The student may recall that the slope of the total product curve is the marginal product. More will be said of this relationship after Chapter 3, "Differentiation," presents the first derivative.

5. This method will return the maximum of average product because the slope of *any* line drawn through the origin and touching a point on the total product curve is the average product for that point on the total curve. The line that is tangent will return the highest slope among such lines.

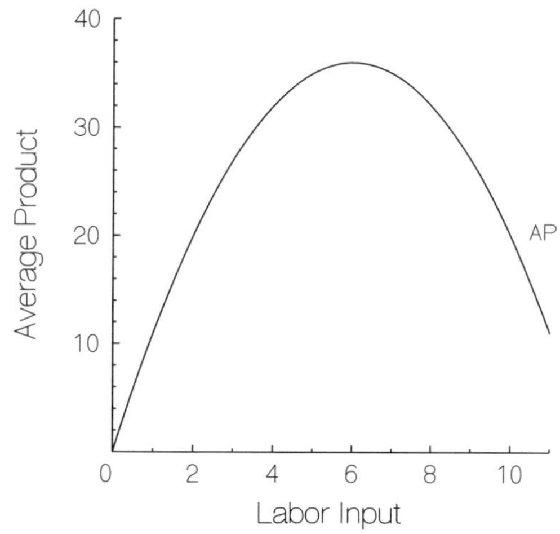

Figure 2-6
The average product function.

2-3 A Nonlinear Demand and Supply Application

All of the demand and supply curves described in section 2-1, "Linear Demand and Supply Curves," are linear. These "curves" are presumed to be linear as a convenience. Solutions to nonlinear relationships are by necessity more difficult, but some may be solved by the relatively simple techniques presented in Chapter 1. Suppose we have the following demand and supply equations for contact lenses, where P is in dollars and Q is in millions of pairs of lenses per month:

$$P = 402 - 3Q_d^2 \qquad (2\text{-}10)$$

$$P = 12 + 9Q_S \qquad (2\text{-}11)$$

The demand curve (Equation 2-10) is a quadratic, whereas the supply curve is linear. Following the same procedure as described in section 2-1, equilibrium requires $Q_d = Q_S$, so the subscripts can be dropped from the Q's. Also, because there is a single price P, we can write the following:

$$402 - 3Q^2 = 12 + 9Q$$

and

$$3Q^2 + 9Q - 390 = 0 \qquad (2\text{-}12)$$

Now Equation 2-12 is of the form $ax^2 + bx + c$, the only difference being that the x's are of course Q's. The solution can be found by factoring, which would involve a lot of guesswork, or by the *quadratic formula*, introduced as Equation 1-7 in Chapter 1 and repeated here:

$$x = \frac{-b \pm \sqrt{b^2 - 4ac}}{2a}$$

The values for a, b, and c may be substituted into the quadratic formula as follows:

$$x = \frac{-9 \pm \sqrt{9^2 - 4(3)(-390)}}{2(3)}$$

which simplifies to

$$x = \frac{-9 \pm \sqrt{4761}}{6} = \frac{-9 \pm 69}{6}$$

so that the solution values are x = –13 and x = 10. These are the values for Q, or the possible solution values for equilibrium quantity. Since negative quantities supplied and demanded have no meaning in economics, we can decide with confidence that the correct equilibrium quantity is 10 (millions of pairs of lenses). The equilibrium price can now be found by substituting 10 into either the demand equation, Equation 2-10, or the supply equation, Equation 2-11. The result is an equilibrium price of $102. The graphic solution of the demand and supply equations is depicted in Figure 2-7.

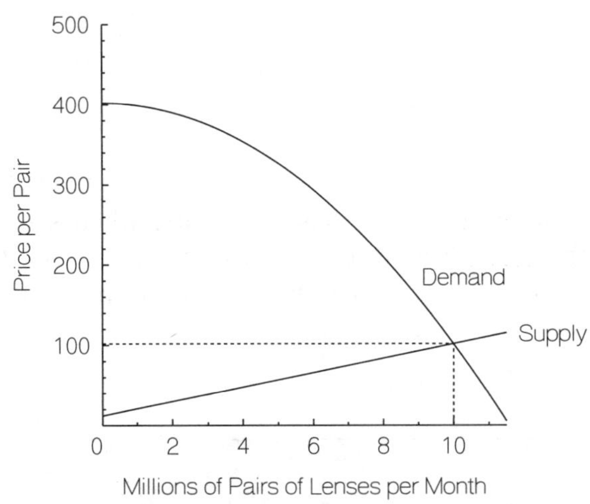

Figure 2-7
A nonlinear demand and supply application.

2-4 A Budget Line

Budget lines, in one form or another, appear throughout microeconomics and all other courses in economics. They are essential for understanding the concept of a constraint; for example, a limitation on the amounts of goods or services that can be purchased in utility analysis. A simple example of a linear budget line is presented here.

Suppose Leonardo has $96 each month to spend on pizza and a designer water called Fizzle. Suppose further that the price of pizza is $8 per pie and bottles of Fizzle are $2 each. Leonardo will spend all of the $96 on these two commodities. A general equation for this relationship is as follows:

$$I = P_pQ_p + P_wQ_w \qquad (2\text{-}13)$$

where

$I = \$96$, the income to be allocated between the two goods

$P_p = \$8$, the price of each pizza

Q_p = the quantity of pizza purchased, a variable

$P_w = \$2$, the price of each bottle of Fizzle water

Q_w = the number of bottles of Fizzle water purchased, a variable

The logic of Equation 2-13 is simply that if Leonardo is to spend his entire income on these two goods, then the price paid for a pizza multiplied by the quantity of pizzas purchased *plus* the price of a bottle of water multiplied by the number of bottles must equal the $96 to be spent on the two goods. Leonardo's budget line is then as follows:

$$\$96 = \$8Q_p + \$2Q_w$$

This is a straight-line function. If we solve for either of the variables, Q_p or Q_w, a more familiar straight-line form will result. Solving for Q_p, this is the general result from Equation 2-13:

$$Q_p = I/P_p - (P_w/P_p)Q_w \qquad (2\text{-}14)$$

The student should be able to recognize that I/P_p is the vertical intercept and $-P_w/P_p$ is the slope of the equation. The specific equation, using the income and prices from above, is as follows:

$$Q_p = 12 - \tfrac{1}{4}Q_w \qquad (2\text{-}15)$$

So the vertical intercept is 12, and the slope is $-\frac{1}{4}$. The student may want to verify that if we had chosen to solve for Q_w, the intercept would have been 48 and the slope –4.

Suppose we want to find the maximum amount of pizza Leonardo could purchase if he purchased no Fizzle water at all. Simply set $Q_w = 0$ in Equation 2-15 and $Q_p = 12$ will be the solution. This is the vertical intercept (see Figure 2-8) and should make intuitive sense because it is income divided by the price of pizza, the first term to the right of the equals sign in Equation 2-14. If Leonardo were to buy only bottles of Fizzle water, how many of those could he buy? The student probably already knows the answer. Simply set $Q_p = 0$ in Equation 2-15 and solve for Q_w. The result is

$$0 = 12 - \tfrac{1}{4}Q_w$$

or

$$\tfrac{1}{4}Q_w = 12$$

and finally

$$Q_w = 48$$

which is the horizontal intercept in Figure 2-8.

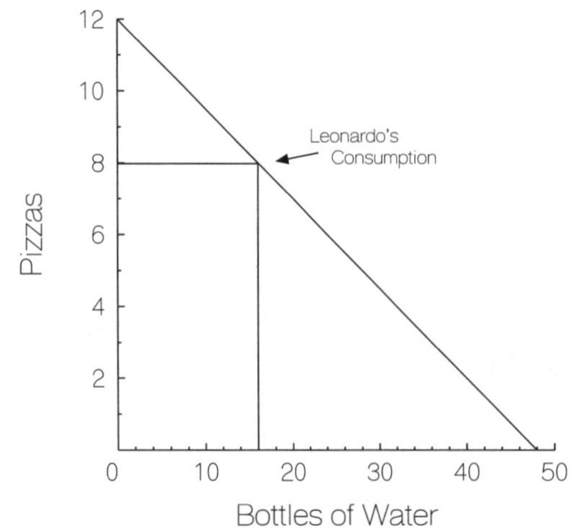

Figure 2-8
A budget line.

As a final problem, suppose for reasons of his own Leonardo always purchases twice as many bottles of Fizzle water as pizzas. How many pizzas and bottles of water will he purchase per month? This solution is found by recognizing that $Q_w = 2Q_p$, and replacing the Q_w in Equation 2-15 with $2Q_p$:

$$Q_p = 12 - \tfrac{1}{4}(2Q_p)$$

so that

$$Q_p = 12 - \tfrac{1}{2}Q_p$$

and

$$Q_p = 8$$

Since $Q_p = 8$, we can substitute this result into Equation 2-15 and find $Q_w = 16$, which we already knew because Q_w is twice Q_p.

2-5 Summary

This chapter has provided several microeconomic applications of equations and graphs. Hopefully, the type of analysis presented here will be helpful to the student as he or she begins to work the numerous problems that are typically assigned in the first few weeks of the semester of the microeconomics course. In addition, a number of problems appear at the end of this chapter. The student is encouraged to work these problems. (Solutions are provided at the end of the book.)

Problems

1. Unlike his father, George W. might like broccoli. In fact suppose the First Family spends \$12 per month on broccoli, regardless of the price of the broccoli.

   (a) Assuming that price is in dollars per pound and quantity is in pounds per month, write the Bush family's demand equation for broccoli.
   (b) Find the quantity demanded for the Bush family for P = \$2 and for P = \$4.
   (c) Find the Bush family's price elasticity of demand for broccoli. (You can do this in more than one way.)

2. Suppose the U.S. market demand for broccoli is such that \$12 million is spent on broccoli each month, regardless of the price. Suppose also that the market supply of broccoli is given by the equation $P = Q_S$.

   (a) Find the equilibrium price and quantity in this market.

   Suppose Congress (see problem 1 above) passes a federal excise tax of \$4 per pound on the lovely green stuff.

   (b) Write the market supply equation after the tax is imposed.
   (c) Find the new equilibrium price and quantity after the tax is imposed.
   (d) How is the tax divided between the buyer and the seller?
   (e) How much less broccoli will be served per month at the dinner table? (Go back to the Bush's demand equation in problem 1.)

3. Consider the short-run total-cost function given by $TC = 10 + 10q - 5q^2 + q^3$, where TC is the total cost (in thousands of dollars) of Mickey Mouse watches and q represents output (in thousands of watches) for this firm.

   (a) Write the equation for fixed cost.
   (b) Write the equation for average total cost.
   (c) Write the equation for average variable cost.
   (d) It can easily be shown that the marginal cost equation implied by the total cost function above is $MC = 3q^2 - 10q + 10$. Given MC, find the minimum values for average variable cost. (Hint: Marginal cost equals average cost at the minimum of average cost. Why?)

4. Assume the short-run cost function in problem 3 applies, including the marginal cost function, $3q^2 - 10q + 10$. Suppose all the watches the firm can make can be sold for \$20 each. The total revenue function is then $TR = 20q$. As stated in Chapter 1, marginal revenue is the *slope* of total revenue; hence, $MR = 20$. As you already know, profit maximization for the firm requires that $MR = MC$.

   (a) Find the output that maximizes profit. (There will be two answers, but only one will be an economic solution.)
   (b) Given the profit maximizing output, find total cost, total revenue, and profit for the firm.

5. You have \$1,000 dollars per year to spend on compact discs (CDs) and video movies. The price of CDs is \$10 each and movies can be purchased for \$20 each.

   (a) Write the equation for the budget line implied by the income and prices stated above, and draw the graph.
   (b) If you choose to purchase 25 videos, how many CDs will you be able to purchase? Show your work mathematically and diagrammatically.

   Due to a recession, you must reduce your expenditures on CDs and movies. You decide to spend only \$750 on these items. There is good news, however. Though the price of CDs has not changed, video movies now cost only \$10.

   (c) Write the equation for the new budget line and draw the graph.
   (d) Show that the combination of CDs and movies that you purchased in part (b) can still be purchased on the budget line that pertains to the recessionary period.

(e) Suppose CDs and movies are neither perfect complements nor perfect substitutes (the indifference curves are "normally" shaped). Show, under these conditions, that you are better off in the recessionary period with respect to CD and movie consumption. (Hint: Draw both budget lines on the same graph and an indifference curve tangent at the point implied by your answer to part (b). You should be able to show that a higher indifference curve can be reached during the recession.)

6. The market demand and supply curves for 10-year-old Mercedes-Benz automobiles are approximated by the following:

$P = 10e^{2Q}$ (supply)

and

$P = 25000e^{-.5Q}$ (demand)

where P = price in dollars, Q = number of cars per month in hundreds of units, and e is the base of the natural logarithms. Find the equilibrium price and quantity. (Hint: Use the rules of logarithms in the appendix to Chapter 1.)

Chapter 3

Differentiation

This chapter presents the techniques of differentiation. Relatively nontechnical discussions of limits and continuity are presented as a part of the development of the derivative of functions of a single variable. Rules are presented for both simple and partial differentiation. In addition, brief treatment is given to differentials and total derivatives.

Outline

3-1 The Derivative of Functions of One Variable

As a student of economics, you have already encountered the concept of a derivative. The *derivative* of a function is the rate of change of that function. In microeconomics, the rate of change of total revenue is marginal revenue, the rate of change of total product is marginal product, and the rate of change of total utility is marginal utility. You may also already know that marginal revenue, product, and utility are defined as the *slope* of their respective total functions. In Chapter 1, the slope of a straight line was defined and methods were presented for its measurement. Derivatives allow us to find the slopes of nonlinear functions, such as the general forms of total revenue, product, and utility.

In Chapter 2, the following demand curve was presented as Equation 2-1:

$$P = 100 - 2Q_d$$

A total revenue (or expenditure) function can be produced for this equation by simply multiplying the equation by Q, since total revenue is price times quantity. Dropping the d subscript, the revenue equation would be as follows:

$$R = 100Q - 2Q^2$$

where R is total revenue and Q can be considered an output rate for an industry or a firm. To make this discussion more general, let's write the equation as shown in Equation 3-1:

$$y = 100x - 2x^2 \qquad (3\text{-}1)$$

The graph of Equation 3-1 (see Figure 3-1) is consistent with what we would expect a revenue function to look like, assuming that the demand curve was linear. Now suppose we are interested in the slope of the total revenue curve at the point $P(x_1, y_1)$.[1] We define another point on the curve, $S(x_2, y_2)$. The straight line drawn between P and S is called a *secant line*. The slope of this secant line is as follows:

$$\textit{slope of PS} = \frac{\Delta y}{\Delta x} = \frac{y_2 - y_1}{x_2 - x_1}$$

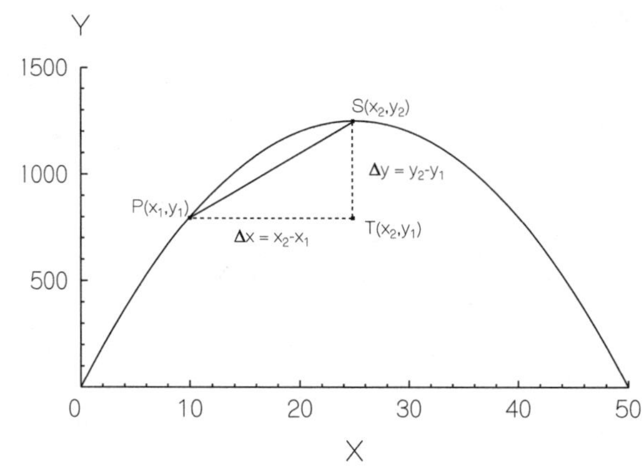

Figure 3-1
A total revenue function.

1. These are regular Cartesian coordinates; that is, $P(x_1, y_1)$ is a point in the x,y space defined by the actual values of x and y. In this case, x = 10 and y = 800.

If P is held in place and we move S closer and closer to P, the slope of the secant line varies. In this case, the slope will remain positive and become larger (steeper). For most curves encountered in practice, as S moves closer and closer to P, the slope of each secant line varies from each previous one by smaller amounts, approaching a constant limiting value. That limiting value is equal to the slope of a tangent at point P (as you may have already known or guessed), which is also the slope of the curve at point P.

We can now demonstrate this powerful fact mathematically. Consider again Equation 3-1:

$$y = 100x - 2x^2$$

Again define two points on the curve, $P(x_1, y_1)$ and $S(x_2, y_2)$. Since $P(x_1, y_1)$ is on the curve, it follows in Equation 3-2 that

$$y_1 = 100x_1 - 2x_1^2 \qquad (3\text{-}2)$$

That is, if the value of x_1 is substituted into Equation 3-1, it must equal y_1. Also, we may now define Δx and Δy, as in the graph:

$$\Delta x = x_2 - x_1$$

and

$$\Delta y = y_2 - y_1$$

It then follows that

$$x_2 = x_1 + \Delta x$$

and

$$y_2 = y_1 + \Delta y$$

These definitions for x_2 and y_2 must also satisfy Equation 3-1. Substituting the right-hand definitions of x_2 and y_2, we have the following equation:

$$y_1 + \Delta y = 100(x_1 + \Delta x) - 2(x_1 + \Delta x)^2$$

Expanding the squared term, and multiplying by the 100, we get this result:

$$y_1 + \Delta y = 100x_1 + 100\Delta x - 2[x_1^2 + 2x_1\Delta x + (\Delta x)^2]$$

or Equation 3-3:

$$y_1 + \Delta y = 100x_1 + 100\Delta x - 2x_1^2 - 4x_1\Delta x - 2(\Delta x)^2 \qquad (3\text{-}3)$$

Now subtract Equation 3-2 from Equation 3-3 to obtain Equation 3-4:

$$\Delta y = 100\Delta x - 4x_1\Delta x - 2(\Delta x)^2 \tag{3-4}$$

Next, divide both sides of Equation 3-4 by Δx to get Equation 3-5:

$$\frac{\Delta y}{\Delta x} = 100 - 4x_1 - 2\Delta x = \textit{slope of PS} \tag{3-5}$$

Recall that we were to allow the point S to approach P along the curve. As this happens, both Δx and Δy become smaller and smaller; they are said to approach zero. Then the slope of PS is the ratio of two small numbers, but we do not know yet what their ratio equals. Additional useful information is at our disposal, however. Examination of Equation 3-5 reveals that the term 2Δx becomes smaller as Δx approaches zero. Indeed, the term must approach zero as well, since zero times any number is also zero. Given this, the slope of PS reduces to this result as Δx approaches zero:

$$\textit{slope of PS} = \frac{\Delta y}{\Delta x} = 100 - 4x_1$$

A formal statement based on this analysis may be made: *The limit of the slope of the secant line as Δx approaches zero is* $100 - 4x_1$. This is also known as the derivative of the original function, $y = 100x - 2x^2$. It is so named because it was *derived* from the original function.

In the example above, the point P is where $x_1 = 10$, so the slope of the function at this point is 100 – 4(10) = 60. Returning to the revenue concept, total revenue is 800 when output is 10. Marginal revenue, the slope of total revenue, is 60 when output is 10.

As a final point in this discussion, recognize that the point P was chosen arbitrarily, hence it could have been anywhere on the curve. This allows us to drop the subscripts on the derivative equation and write simply that, as Δx approaches zero,

$$\frac{\Delta y}{\Delta x} = 100 - 4x$$

3-1a A Generalization

The results of section 3-1 can be generalized. In defining a derivative for a function, y = f(x), we want to find the ratio of Δy/Δx as Δx approaches zero. The general form of the derivative may be written as shown in Equation 3-6:

$$\lim_{\Delta x \to 0} \frac{\Delta y}{\Delta x} = \lim_{\Delta x \to 0} \frac{f(x + \Delta x) - f(x)}{\Delta x} \tag{3-6}$$

Rather than the cumbersome expression to the left of the equals sign, it is conventional to designate the derivative as dy/dx, so that the generalized expression becomes that shown in Equation 3-7:

$$\frac{dy}{dx} = \lim_{\Delta x \to 0} \frac{f(x + \Delta x) - f(x)}{\Delta x} \tag{3-7}$$

The reader should recognize that other conventions are used for expressing the derivative. The symbols y' and $f'(x)$ are also frequently used to express the derivative of the function $y = f(x)$.

Several points should be emphasized in reference to the *difference quotient* written either as Equation 3-6 or 3-7. The difference in the numerator on the right-hand side of the equals sign is obtained by evaluating the function at two values, namely at x and at $x + \Delta x$. Then the difference between these values yields Δy. Two restrictions must apply with regard to Δx. First, the function must be defined for $x + \Delta x$. Second, as implied above, Δx cannot be zero, since that would require division by zero, which violates the conventions of algebra. The symbol

$$\lim_{\Delta x \to 0}$$

means, "The limit of ... as Δx approaches zero." If the limit of the difference quotient exists as Δx approaches zero, that limit is the derivative of the function $y = f(x)$.

In summary, we find the slope of a function at a point by finding the derivative of the function and evaluating the derivative for the value of x at that point on the function. Finding the derivative involves the *difference quotient* from Equation 3-6 or 3-7 and requires the evaluation of a limit.

3-1b A Brief Digression on Limits and Continuity

Following is a useful definition of a limit:

> The limit of a function exists if and only if the left-hand and right-hand limits exist, are identical, and are equal to some finite value.

The *left-hand* and *right-hand* terms mean that, in evaluating the limit of a function at some value, say x, x may be approached from values greater than x (the right-hand side), or from values less than x (the left-hand side). The last part of the definition, that the limit has to be finite, is actually debatable. Some mathematicians are willing to speak of the limit of a function as plus or minus infinity. Let's side with those who argue that since infinity is limitless, it should not be called a *limit.* In microeconomics, most (but not all) functions have limits, at least in the range in which we want to evaluate them.

Because most functions that the student encounters in microeconomics have limits where we want to evaluate them, let's examine two cases where limits would not exist. To facilitate this discussion, I need to introduce the concept of continuity.

To be *continuous* at a value in the domain[2] (call this value c), a function (call this function f(x)) must meet three requirements:

1. f(x) is defined for c.
2. The function must have a limit as x approaches c.
3. This limit is equal to the value of the function at c.

This is a rather formal definition. A more intuitive explanation of continuity is that a function is continuous on an interval if the graph of the function is an unbroken curve on that interval. That is, the curve could be drawn on that interval without lifting the pen or pencil from the paper.

2. The domain is all permissible values for x for the function f(x).

3-1c The Relationship Between Limits, Continuity, and Derivatives

The most appealing explanations of the relationship between limits, continuity, and differentiability utilize examples to make the connections. This section looks at four graphs that will cover most of the cases you are likely to encounter. Let's set forth a proposition that defines differentiability:

Assume y = f(x). If the limit

$$\frac{dy}{dx} = \lim_{\Delta x \to 0} \frac{f(x + \Delta x) - f(x)}{\Delta x}$$

exists and is finite, this limit is called the derivative of y with respect to x and the function y = f(x) is said to be differentiable at x.

Armed with this definition, reconsider the function shown in Figure 3-1. The function is continuous everywhere (an unbroken curve). The limit of the difference quotient (refer to Equation 3-7) also would exist everywhere, since the limit would be the same if approached from the left or right, and this limit would be finite. The derivative of the function exists for all values of x.

Consider a function that is not continuous. Let y = f(x) = [x] = the largest integer in x. This is the so-called *step function* depicted in Figure 3-2. This function has discontinuities at every integer value; the pen or pencil must be lifted to get to the next step. Consider the value of the function as $x \to 2$. If x approaches 2 from the right, the limit is 2, but if x approaches 2 from the left, the limit is 1. The left-hand and right-hand limits exist but are not identical, hence the limit of f(x) does not exist. What we have shown so far is that the function does not have a limit at x = 2. It can be shown that if the original function (also known as the *primitive* function) does not have a limit at this point, the limit of the difference quotient ($\Delta y/\Delta x$) as $\Delta x \to 0$ cannot exist at this point either. Recognize that we are referring to limits at two levels here. The first limit is that of the primitive function itself and the second limit is that of the difference quotient for that primitive. The point is that, if the first limit, the limit of the *primitive* function, y = f(x), does not exist at a value c, then the second limit, the limit of the difference quotient as $\Delta x \to 0$ at c, will not exist either. This second limit, if it does exist, is the derivative. It then follows that the function in Figure 3-2 is not differentiable at x = 2, or at any of the other values of x where the "step" occurs.

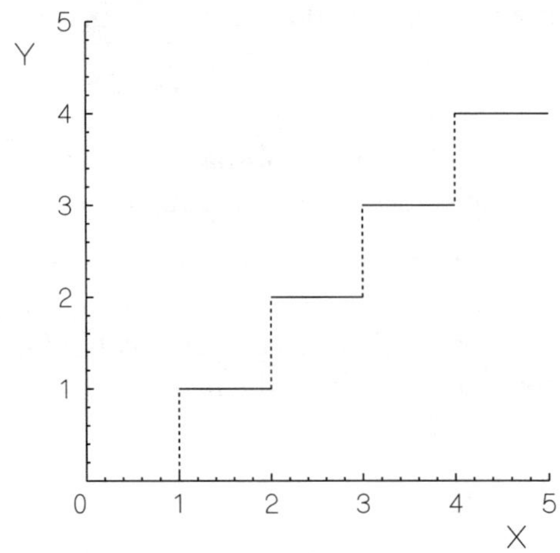

Figure 3-2
A step function.

Consider a function that has another type of discontinuity. Figure 3-3 is the graph of the function y = f(x) = 1/x. Since division by zero is not permissible, the first requirement for continuity, that f(x) is defined, is violated at x = 0. The function must be discontinuous at this point. Additionally, as x→0 from the right, the limit approaches +∞, and as x→0 from the left, the function approaches –∞. By our criteria, the limit does not exist because the left-hand and right-hand limits are not finite, nor are they identical. Finally, consider the limit of the difference quotient at x = 0. We can easily see that Δy/Δx, the slope of the function, will also approach +∞ or –∞, depending on the direction from which Δx approaches zero, confirming that the derivative does not exist at x = 0. So neither the limit of the primitive function nor the limit of the difference quotient exist for y = 1/x, at x = 0.

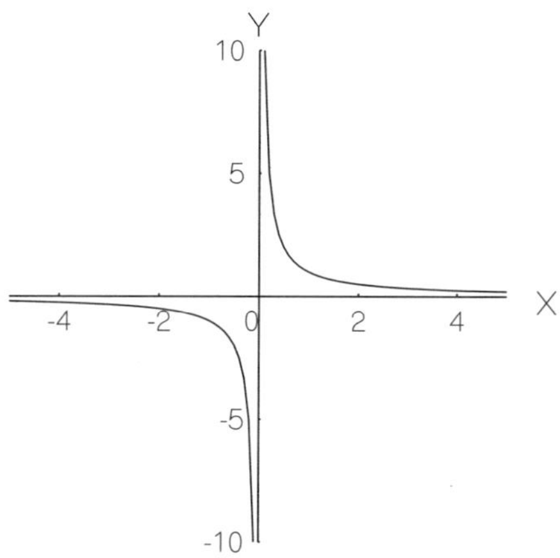

Figure 3-3
A hyperbola.

You may be thinking at this point that a function must be continuous in order to be differentiable. That is correct. If you are thinking also that all continuous functions are differentiable, you have been tricked by the old "necessary but not sufficient" condition. Continuity of the primitive function is necessary for the function to be differentiable, but many continuous functions are not differentiable. In other words, continuity of a function at a point does not ensure (is not a sufficient condition for) differentiability. To show this, consider the function in Figure 3-4, y = |x| + 1.

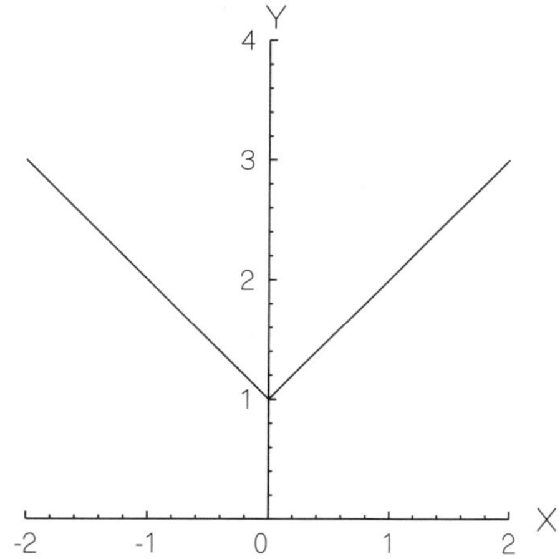

Figure 3-4
The function y = |x| + 1.

This function meets the three criteria for continuity at the point where x = 0. However, the function does not possess a derivative at x = 0. The reason that the derivative does not exist at this point is that the derivative, or slope of the function, will equal –1 as Δx approaches 0 from the left, but as Δx approaches 0 from the right, the slope equals +1. Therefore, since the difference quotient does not produce a unique value from the left and right, a limit does not exist for the difference quotient and hence there is no derivative for the function at x = 0. The mathematics of this result are as follows:

$$\frac{f(0 + \Delta x) - f(0)}{\Delta x} = \frac{|\Delta x|}{\Delta x}$$

and

$$\frac{|\Delta x|}{\Delta x} = 1$$

when Δx > 0,

$$\frac{|\Delta x|}{\Delta x} = -1$$

when Δx < 0. Therefore,

$$\lim_{\Delta x \to 0} \frac{|\Delta x|}{\Delta x}$$

does not exist.

Again, the derivative would find the slope of the curve or a tangent to the curve at that point. A simple way to tell that no derivative exists at x = 0 is to note that you could draw many tangents to the function at this point.

Where does this leave us as to the relationship between continuity, limits, and differentiability? Let's summarize three main points:

- A function must be continuous to be differentiable, but it does not follow that all continuous functions are differentiable.
- Limits must exist at two levels for a function to be differentiable at a value c: The limit of f(x) must exist at c *and* the limit of the difference quotient, Δy/Δx as Δx→0, must also exist at c.
- To be differentiable, a function must be continuous *and* it must also be *smooth*; that is, it must not have a sharp change in slope, as in Figure 3-4.

As stated earlier, in undergraduate microeconomics you will encounter few functions that are not differentiable everywhere. Those that are not differentiable everywhere can usually be handled in a relatively simple manner.

3-2 Rules for Derivatives

This section states 10 rules for finding derivatives. Whereas the previous section was somewhat technical and theoretical, this section is mechanical. No proofs are offered, but rest assured that such proofs exist, and they may be found in many books dedicated to calculus or mathematical economics. Here we merely state rules and examples.

Rule 1. *The derivative of a constant is zero.* Given a function y = c, where c is some constant, then:

$$\frac{dy}{dx} = 0$$

regardless of the value of x, since the value of the function is still equal to the constant. Hence, the effect of a change in x on the value of y is zero. Also, the graph of a constant is a horizontal line, a line parallel to the x axis (see Figure 1-1, Chapter 1) and the slope (or derivative) of a horizontal line is zero.

Examples

1. If $y = 6$, $\frac{dy}{dx} = 0$
2. If $y = 100$, $\frac{dy}{dx} = 0$
3. If $y = -25$, $\frac{dy}{dx} = 0$
4. If $FC = \$100$, $\frac{d(FC)}{dq} = 0$

Example 4 shows that if fixed cost (FC) is \$100, fixed costs do not change when output (q) changes.

Rule 2. *The derivative of x^n with respect to x is nx^{n-1}, where n is any real number.*

Examples

1. If $y = x$, $\frac{dy}{dx} = 1$ (since $1x^{1-1} = x^0$ and $x^0 = 1$)
2. If $y = x^2$, $\frac{dy}{dx} = 2x$
3. If $y = x^3$, $\frac{dy}{dx} = 3x^2$
4. If $y = x^{-2}$, $\frac{dy}{dx} = -2x^{-3}$
5. If $y = x^{88}$, $\frac{dy}{dx} = 88x^{87}$

Rule 3. *The derivative of a constant times a function is the constant times the derivative of the function.* Let u = f(x) and c be a constant, such that y = cu. Then:

$$\frac{d(cu)}{dx} = c\,\frac{du}{dx}$$

Rules 2 and 3 together allow us to find derivatives for expressions such as $y = 3x^4$, where $c = 3$, and $u = x^4$, and $y = cu$. Then:

$$\frac{du}{dx} = 4x^3 \text{and } c\,\frac{du}{dx} = 12x^3 = \frac{dy}{dx}$$

Examples

1. If $y = 4x,\ \frac{dy}{dx} = 4$
2. If $y = 7x^3,\ \frac{dy}{dx} = (7)(3)x^2 = 21x^2$
3. If $y = 10x^{1/2},\ \frac{dy}{dx} = (10)(1/2)x^{-1/2} = 5x^{-1/2}$
4. If $y = 3x^{-2},\ \frac{dy}{dx} = (3)(-2)x^{-3} = -6x^{-3}$

Rule 4. *The derivative of the sum (or difference) of two functions is the sum (or difference) of the two derivatives.* Let $u = f(x)$ and $v = g(x)$ so that $y = u + v$ or ($y = u - v$). Then:

$$\frac{dy}{dx} = \frac{d(u+v)}{dx} = \frac{du}{dx} + \frac{dv}{dx}$$

and

$$\frac{dy}{dx} = \frac{d(u-v)}{dx} = \frac{du}{dx} - \frac{dv}{dx}$$

Examples

1. If $y = 10 + 20x - 3x^2,\ \frac{dy}{dx} = 20 - 6x$
2. If $y = mx + b,\ \frac{dy}{dx} = m$
3. If $y = 20 + 10x - 3x^2 + 12x^3,\ \frac{dy}{dx} = 10 - 6x + 36x^2$

Rule 5. *The derivative of the product of two functions is the first function times the derivative of the second plus the second function times the derivative of the first.* Let $u = f(x)$ and $v = g(x)$ so that $y = uv$. Then:

$$\frac{dy}{dx} = (u)\frac{dv}{dx} + (v)\frac{du}{dx}$$

Examples

1. If $y = x^3(2x + 10)$, $\dfrac{dy}{dx} = x^3(2) + (2x + 10)(3x^2) = 8x^3 + 30x^2$
2. If $y = (x^2 + 4)(5x^4 - 5)$

   $$\frac{dy}{dx} = (x^2 + 4)(20x^3) + (5x^4 - 5)(2x) = 30x^5 + 80x^3 - 10x$$
3. If $y = (x^3 + 2x^2)(5x - 2x^4)$

   $$\frac{dy}{dx} = (x^3 + 2x^2)(5 - 8x^3) + (5x - 2x^4)(3x^2 + 4x)$$

   $$= -14x^6 - 24x^5 + 20x^3 + 30x^2$$

Rule 6. *The derivative of the quotient of two functions is equal to the denominator times the derivative of the numerator minus the numerator times the derivative of the denominator, all divided by the square of the denominator.* Let u = f(x) and v = g(x) so that y = u/v. Then:

$$\frac{dy}{dx} = \frac{(v)\dfrac{du}{dx} - (u)\dfrac{dv}{dx}}{v^2}$$

Examples

1. If $y = (x^2 - 3x + 2)/(x - 5)$

   $$\frac{dy}{dx} = \frac{(x - 5)(2x - 3) - (x^2 - 3x + 2)(1)}{(x - 5)^2}$$

   $$\frac{dy}{dx} = \frac{x^2 - 10x + 13}{(x - 5)^2}$$
2. If $y = 1/x^2$

   $$\frac{dy}{dx} = \frac{(x^2)(0) - (1)(2x)}{(x^2)^2} = \frac{-2x}{x^4} = \frac{-2}{x^3}$$
3. In general, if $y = 1/x^n$

   $$\frac{dy}{dx} = \frac{(x^n)(0) - (1)(nx^{n-1})}{(x^n)^2} = -\frac{nx^{n-1}}{x^{2n}} = -\frac{n}{x^{n+1}}$$

4. *If* $y = (2x + 1) / (x^2 - 1)$

$$\frac{dy}{dx} = \frac{(x^2 - 1)(2) - (2x + 1)(2x)}{(x^2 - 1)^2}$$

$$\frac{dy}{dx} = \frac{-2x^2 - 2x - 2}{(x^2 - 1)^2} = \frac{-2(x^2 + x + 1)}{(x^2 - 1)^2}$$

Rule 7. *If y is a function of u and u is a function of x, then y is a composite function; that is, a function of a function. The derivative of y with respect to x is the product of the derivative of y with respect to u and the derivative of u with respect to x.* This rule is called either *the chain rule* or the *composite function rule.* Let $y = f(u)$ and $u = g(x)$, so that $y = f[g(x)]$. Then:

$$\frac{dy}{dx} = \frac{dy}{du} \bullet \frac{du}{dx}$$

Examples

1. *If* $y = u^2$ *and* $u = 3x^2 + 5$, *so that* $y = (3x^2 + 5)^2$

$$\frac{dy}{dx} = 2(3x^2 + 5)(6x) = 36x^3 + 60x, \text{ since}$$

$$\frac{dy}{du} = 2u = 2(3x^2 + 5) \text{ and}$$

$$\frac{du}{dx} = 6x$$

2. *If* $y = u - 10$ *and* $u = x^4$, *so that* $y = x^4 - 10$

$$\frac{dy}{dx} = (1)(4x^3) = 4x^3$$

3. *If* $y = (2x^2 + 4x - 10)^8$, *let* $y = u^8$ *and* $u = 2x^2 + 4x - 10$, *then*

$$\frac{dy}{du} = 8u^7 = 8(2x^2 + 4x - 10)^7$$

and

$$\frac{du}{dx} = 4x + 4$$

therefore

$$\frac{du}{dx} = 8(2x^2 + 4x - 10)^7(4x + 4)$$

Example 3 is the most useful type of application of this rule because it is possible to avoid multiplying out the 8th power expression.

3-2a Implicit Differentiation

In Rules 1–7, the form of each function is written y = f(x); that is, y is an explicit function of x. Some functions are written as implicit functions, f(x,y) = 0, and some of these cannot be *solved* for y. But if a specific number is substituted for x, these relationships will define one or more values of y, and are, therefore, called *implicit functions* of x. The method used to find the derivative of these functions is called (you guessed it!) *implicit differentiation.* To apply this method, we simply treat y as an unknown but differentiable function of x and apply Rules 1–7 to each term in the equation.

Rule 8. *If y is defined as an implicit function of x, the derivative of y with respect to x is found by differentiating the equation f(x,y) = 0, term by term, considering y as a function of x, and solving the resulting expression for the derivative, dy/dx.*

Examples

1. *If* $x^2 + y^2 - 1 = 0$, *differentiating implicitly gives*

$$2x + 2y\frac{dy}{dx} + 0 = 0$$

$$\frac{dy}{dx} = -\frac{x}{y}$$

Note: This derivative applies the composite function rule, Rule 7. (See example 1 under rule 7.) The derivative of the term:

$$y^2 = 2y\frac{dy}{dx}$$

because y is a function of x. If we have u^n, and u = f(x), then:

$$\frac{dy}{dx} = nu^{n-1}\frac{du}{dx}$$

Here we have y^n and y = f(x).

2. *If* $x^3 + y^4 - 2xy = 0$, *differentiating implicitly gives:*

$$3x^2 + 4y^3\frac{dy}{dx} - 2x\frac{dy}{dx} - 2y = 0$$

$$(4y^3 - 2x)\frac{dy}{dx} = 2y - 3x^2$$

$$\frac{dy}{dx} = \frac{2y - 3x^2}{4y^3 - 2x}$$

3. *If* $x^4 + 3xy^3 - 2y^5 = 0$, *differentiating implicitly gives:*

$$4x^3 + 3(3xy^2 \frac{dy}{dx} + y^3) - 10y^4 \frac{dy}{dx} = 0$$

$$\frac{dy}{dx}(9xy^2 - 10y^4) = -(4x^3 + 3y^3)$$

$$\frac{dy}{dx} = \frac{4x^3 - 3y^3}{10y^4 - 9xy^2}$$

Note: The part of the expression xy^3 is treated as uv in the product rule, with u = x and v = y^3.

3-2b Derivatives of Logarithmic and Exponential Functions[3]

Logarithmic Functions

Recall from Chapter 1 that e is the base of the natural logarithms and is approximately equal to 2.71828. We will consider only the derivatives of natural logarithms.

Rule 9. *If y is defined as the natural log of u, and u is a function of x, the derivative of y with respect to x is the reciprocal of u times the derivative of u with respect to x.* Let y = ln u, and u = f(x), then:

$$\frac{dy}{dx} = \frac{1}{u} \bullet \frac{du}{dx}$$

Examples

---

1. *If* $y = \ln x$

$$\frac{dy}{dx} = \frac{1}{x} \bullet 1 = \frac{1}{x}$$

2. *If* $y = \ln(2x^2 - 3x)$

$$\frac{dy}{dx} = \frac{1}{2x^2 - 3x} \bullet (4x - 3)$$

$$\frac{dy}{dx} = \frac{4x - 3}{x(2x - 3)}$$

3. *If* $y = (\ln x)/x$

$$\frac{dy}{dx} = \frac{(\frac{1}{x})x - \ln x}{x^2}$$

$$\frac{dy}{dx} = \frac{1 - \ln x}{x^2}$$

---

3. This section may be omitted without loss in continuity.

Exponential Functions

Rule 10: *The derivative of any positive constant a, raised to a variable power u, where u is a differentiable function of x, is equal to the product of the original expression, the natural log of the base, and the derivative of u with respect to x.* Let $y = a^u$, and $u = f(x)$, then:

$$\frac{dy}{dx} = a^u \ln a \frac{du}{dx}$$

Examples

1. If $y = 5^x$

$$\frac{dy}{dx} = 5^x(\ln 5)(1) = 5^x \ln 5$$

2. If $y = 8x^{x^3-2x}$

$$\frac{dy}{dx} = (8^{x3-2x})(\ln^8)(3x^2 - 2)$$

$$\frac{dy}{dx} = (3x^2 - 2)8^{x^3-2x} \ln 8$$

A special case of Rule 10: *If* $y = e^u$, *and u is a differentiable function of x,*

$$\frac{dy}{dx} = e^u \frac{du}{dx}.$$

Examples

1. If $y = e^x$

$$\frac{dy}{dx} = e^x(1) = e^x$$

2. If $y = 100e^{.10x}$

$$\frac{dy}{dx} = 100(e^{.10x})(.10)$$

$$\frac{dy}{dx} = 10e^{.10x}$$

3-3 Partial Differentiation

Few relationships in microeconomics are truly functions of a single variable. We get around this fact by the famous "ceteris paribus" assumption that all other things remain the same. You have already encountered this concept in relation to the demand curve; prices of related goods, income, tastes, and other influences are held constant while we derive a unique relationship between quantity demanded and the price of the good being considered.

Partial derivatives allow us to write functions that more realistically describe economic relationships (multiple variables on the right-hand side) and still capture the effect of a change in only one of the variables on the right-hand side (often called *independent variables*) on the dependent, or left-hand variable. It is necessary to assume that the right-hand causal variables are independent of each other, so that one of them can change and have its effect on the dependent variable without *causing* a change in one of the other independent variables.

Consider a function of the form shown in Equation 3-8

$$y = f(x_1, x_2, \ldots, x_n) \tag{3-8}$$

where y is the dependent variable that "depends" on the independent variables x_1 through x_n. The *partial derivative* of y with respect to x_i, typically represented by $\partial y/\partial x_i$, is defined as the change in y due to the change in x_i, while all other variables are held constant. If the variable that is allowed to change is x_1, the difference quotient for the operation is as shown in Equation 3-9:

$$\frac{\partial y}{\partial x_1} = \lim_{\Delta x_1 \to 0} \frac{f(x_1 + \Delta x_1, x_2, \ldots, x_n) - f(x_1, x_2, \ldots, x_n)}{\Delta x_1} \tag{3-9}$$

Other expressions for the partial derivative include

$$\frac{\partial y}{\partial x_1} = \frac{\partial}{\partial x_1} f(x_1, x_2, \ldots, x_n) = f_1 = f_{x_1} = y_{x_1}$$

We will try to stick with $\partial y/\partial x_1$ as often as possible.

3-3a Rules for Partial Differentiation

We finally get a break here. The rules of differentiation we applied to functions of one variable apply to functions of more than one variable. How exactly is that? In partial differentiation we hold n–1 independent variables constant while allowing only one independent variable to vary. That means that we can treat all of the other variables as if they were, in fact, constants, and we already know how to treat constants in the differentiation process. Let us be clear. Suppose we are differentiating y with respect to x_1. If a term such as $x_2x_3^2$ appears in the equation, it is a constant and its derivative is zero. And, if a term such as $10\,x_4x_1^3$ appears, the $10x_4$ part is a constant and the derivative of this term is simply $30\,x_4x_1^2$.

Examples

1. If $y = f(x_1, x_2) = 5x_1^3 + x_1x_2 + 3x_2^2$

$$\frac{\partial y}{\partial x_1} = 15x_1^2 + x_2$$

(x_2 is treated as a constant attached to x_1 in the second term and the third term, $3x_2^2$ is simply an additive constant or number.)

$$\frac{\partial y}{\partial x_2} = x_1 + 6x_2$$

2. If $y = f(u, v) = (u + 2)(2u^3 + 4v)$, the partial derivatives can be found by use of the product rule:

$$\frac{\partial y}{\partial u} = (u + 2)(6u^2) + (2u^3 + 4v)(1)$$

$$= 8u^3 + 12u^2 + 4v$$

$$\frac{\partial y}{\partial v} = (u+2)(4) + (2u^3 + 4v)(0)$$
$$= 4u + 8$$

3. If $z = f(x, y) = (x^3 - y^3)/xy$, the partials can be found by the quotient rule:

$$\frac{\partial y}{\partial x} = \frac{xy(3x^2) - (x^3 - y^3)(y)}{(xy)^2}$$

$$\frac{\partial z}{\partial x} = 2x^3y(x^{-2}y^{-2}) + y^4(x^{-2}y^{-2})$$
$$= 2xy^{-1} + y^2x^{-2}$$

similarly, for ∂z/∂y,

$$\frac{\partial z}{\partial y} = \frac{xy(-3y^2) - (x^3 - y^3)(x)}{(xy)^2}$$
$$= (-2xy^3 - x^4)(x^{-2}y^{-2})$$

The student should recognize that it is often easier to rewrite the original equation so that a simpler derivative rule can be applied. Example 3 on page 52 can be rewritten like this:

$$z = x^2y^{-1} - y^2x^{-1}$$

and the "sum or difference" rule applies. The student can verify that the same result would pertain. Also, the multiplication implied in the equation in Example 2 may be performed prior to computing the derivative. There are, however, many cases where it is necessary to use the more complicated rules.

3-4 Differentials and Total Derivatives

In this final section of Chapter 3, we develop two important concepts that are useful in economic analysis and that require the knowledge of derivatives of functions considered in sections 3-1 through 3-3.

3-4a Derivatives and Differentials

If y is a function of x (y = f(x)), each time x changes a change in y occurs; that is, Δx brings Δy, and we know that Δy/Δx is the rate of change of y with respect to x. If we know the value of Δy/Δx, and the magnitude Δx, then Δy can be found as shown in Equation 3-10.

$$\Delta y \equiv (\Delta y/\Delta x)(\Delta x) \qquad (3\text{-}10)$$

If Δx→0, and Δy→0 as well, and the difference quotient Δy/Δx will become the derivative dy/dx. Let dy = Δy as Δy→0, and dx = Δx as Δx→0. Then the identity becomes Equation 3-11:

$$dy \equiv (dy/dx)(dx) \qquad (3\text{-}11)$$

where dy is called the differential of y and dx is called the differential of x. Simple manipulation of Equation 3-11 shows that the derivative can be expressed as the ratio of two separable differentials (simply divide both sides of the equation by the differential dx).

The important principle to be gleaned from Equation 3-11 is that the differential dy can be calculated by multiplying the differential dx by the derivative of y with respect to x. That is, for very small changes in x, the corresponding very small change in y can be calculated by using dy/dx as a *converter.* Remember that this works only for very small changes in x unless the function has a constant derivative; that is, y is a linear function of x.

3-4b Total Differentials

When y is a function of more than one variable, for example,

$$y = f(x_1, x_2)$$

the differential of y involves the partial derivatives. The proper expression is shown in Equation 3-12:

$$dy = \frac{\partial y}{\partial x_1} dx_1 + \frac{\partial y}{\partial x_2} dx_2 \qquad (3\text{-}12)$$

which is known as a total differential. The general case for a function of n independent variables and its total differential is

$$y = f(x_1, x_2, \ldots, x_n), \text{ and}$$

$$dy = \frac{\partial y}{\partial x_1} dx_1 + \frac{\partial y}{\partial x_2} dx_2 + \ldots + \frac{\partial y}{\partial x_n} dx_n$$

The rules for differentials follow from the rules for derivatives. Once dy/dx is found, both sides of the derivative equation may be multiplied by dx to define the differential.

3-4c Total Derivatives

In defining partial derivatives, it was assumed that the independent variables were not interrelated. In economics, the "independent" variables are often *dependent* on each other. For example, in utility analysis, satisfaction may be a function of two goods that are themselves complements or substitutes for each other; in other words, they are related goods. In a case such as this, the assumption of independence breaks down. With the concept of a differential now defined, it is possible to ascertain the change in a function with respect to one variable when that variable is related to other right-hand variables.

Consider a function of the type described earlier:

$$y = f(x, z) \text{ where } x = g(z)$$

Now, if z changes, it will have two effects on y: a *direct* effect on y because y is a function of z, and an *indirect* effect on y, since z will cause a change in x which will in turn cause a change in y. To see how to show this via a total derivative, first compute the total differential dy:

$$dy = \frac{\partial y}{\partial x}dx + \frac{\partial y}{\partial z}dz$$

Next, divide both sides of the total differential by dz to obtain Equation 3-13:

$$\frac{dy}{dz} = \frac{\partial y}{\partial x}\frac{dx}{dz} + \frac{\partial y}{\partial z}\frac{dz}{dz}$$

or

$$\frac{dy}{dz} = \frac{\partial y}{\partial x}\frac{dx}{dz} + \frac{\partial y}{\partial z}$$

since $dz/dz = 1$ *(3-13)*

Now the direct effect is the second term on the right, $\partial y/\partial z$, and the indirect effect is the first term on the right, $(\partial y/\partial x)(dx/dz)$. This last expression shows that as z changes (dz), it causes a change in x (dx), which then causes y to change through $\partial y/\partial x$.

Example

If $y = 2x + z^3$ *and* $x = 4z^2 + 10$

$$\frac{dy}{dz} = 2(8z) + 3z^2 = 16z + 3z^2$$

Obviously, since there may be more than two right-hand variables, the interrelationships between variables may be much more complicated. Relationships of this type will produce "chains" of derivatives. Generally, at the undergraduate level in microeconomics these interrelationships are relatively simple, and therefore this simple introduction will suffice.

3-5 Summary

This chapter has presented most of the types of derivatives a student of microeconomics is likely to encounter. Derivations have been presented in simple and intuitive form, as opposed to formal proofs for all of the rules and concepts. It is now time to present some of the applications of the derivative concept to microeconomic examples.

Problems

1. Find the derivative dy/dx of the following:

   (a) $y = 2x$
   (b) $y = 300$
   (c) $y = 3x^2 - 6$
   (d) $y = 2x(x^2 + 3)$
   (e) $y = (3x^2 - x^3)(2x + 4x^5)$
   (f) $y = 6x^2 + 20 - 10$
   (g) $y = (6x + 3x^2)/2x$
   (h) $y = (x^4 - 3x^2)/(x - 3)$
   (i) $y = 2u + 3$, where $u = 6x^2 + 3x$

(j) $y = 2u^2$, where $u = 6 - 2x^2$
(k) $y = (3x^2 - 2x^3 - 10)^4$
(l) $y = \ln(4x^2 + x)$
(m) $y = 2x[\ln(4x^2 + 3x)]$
(n) $y = 2^{(x^2 - 3x + 2)}$
(o) $y = 2e^{2x}$
(p) $y = 3xe^{(2x + 1)}$

2. Use implicit differentiation to find dy/dx for the following:

   (a) $2x^2 - 3y^4 + 4xy^2 = 0$
   (b) $3x^2y^2 + 2xy^2 - 5x^2 + \ln x = 0$

3. Given $z = 2x^4 + 3y^2 - 2xy + 3y$

   (a) find the partial derivative with respect to x
   (b) find the partial derivative with respect to y

4. Given $y = (3u^2 + v)(2v + 5)$

   (a) find the partial derivative with respect to u
   (b) find the partial derivative with respect to v

5. Find the total differential (dz) for the following:

   (a) $z = 2x^2y - xy$
   (b) $z = 5x^2 - 3y^2 + 4xy^2$

6. Find the total derivative dy/dz, given:

   (a) $y = 3x + 2xz - z^2$, where $x = 3z^3 + 4$
   (b) $y = x - xz + 3z^2$, where $x = 10 - z$

7. Find the total derivative du/dx, given:

   (a) $u = x^{.5}y^{.5}$, where $y = 10 - 2x$
   (b) $u = x^2 + xy + 2y^2$, where $100 = x + y$

Chapter 4

Microeconomic Applications of Derivatives

Every text in undergraduate microeconomics is literally filled with applications of the concept of the derivative. Every time the term *marginal* is used (which must seem like every other word), the derivative of some total measure is involved. In this chapter, a number of applications of derivatives are offered. Now that the student is aware of (or reacquainted with) the mechanics and meaning of differentiation, a deeper and fuller appreciation of these applications should result.

Outline

4-1 A Number of Marginal Concepts

Any time we are considering a concept that has the label "total" attached, the economist is typically interested in the corresponding marginal relationship. This is because economic decisions tend to be made at the margin: Should a firm hire one more worker? Should I eat one more donut? Should I go to one more class today? Should I read one more sentence in this book? The decision rests on the sign of the difference between the expected additional benefits and the expected additional costs. If the expected added benefits of reading the next sentence exceed the additional (marginal) cost, you will decide to continue reading. You should already know that the marginal cost of reading one more sentence is the best alternative use of that time.

4-1a Marginal Revenue

In introducing the concept of a derivative, Chapter 3 used a demand curve specified as shown in Equation 4-1:

$$P = 100 - 2Q \qquad (4\text{-}1)$$

Equation 4-2 shows the corresponding total revenue (R) function:

$$R = 100Q - 2Q^2 \text{ (since } R = PQ) \qquad (4\text{-}2)$$

Since marginal revenue is defined as the change in total revenue for a small change in the number of units sold (Q), Equation 4-3 shows another variation:

$$MR = \frac{dR}{dQ} = 100 - 4Q \qquad (4\text{-}3)$$

The relationships between total revenue, demand, and marginal revenue can now be summarized simply:

1. Total revenue can be found from the demand curve by multiplying the demand equation, stated in terms of P, times Q, hence R = PQ. It also follows that the demand curve can be obtained by dividing the total revenue function by Q (P = R/Q). Also note that this formulation produces an *average revenue*, since we divided total revenue by output. A given price is then the average revenue per unit for some specific number of units sold, and most texts in microeconomics use price and average revenue interchangeably.
2. Marginal revenue, the additional revenue from the sale of "one more" unit, or the change in total revenue from "one more" unit sold, is the slope or derivative of the total revenue function.
3. When the demand curve is linear (and downward sloping), marginal revenue has the same vertical intercept and is twice as steep as the demand curve.

This last assertion can be proven simply. Assume a general linear demand curve, as shown in Equation 4-4:

$$P = a - bQ \qquad (4\text{-}4)$$

Then the total revenue function is $R = aQ - bQ^2$. Marginal revenue, the derivative of total revenue, is shown in Equation 4-5:

$$\frac{dR}{dQ} = a - 2bQ \tag{4-5}$$

which has the same vertical intercept and is twice as steep. Also verify that if you solve the demand equation (Equation 4-4) for P = 0 to obtain the horizontal (or Q) intercept, the result is a/b. And if you solve the marginal revenue equation (Equation 4-5) for P = 0 to obtain that horizontal (or Q) intercept, the result is –(a/b). This gives us an easy method for drawing the marginal revenue curve for any linear demand curve: Draw the demand curve intersecting both axes; then draw the marginal revenue curve with the same vertical intercept and one-half the horizontal intercept, as shown in Figure 4-1. These methods for drawing the marginal revenue curve hold only for *linear* demand curves; however, the marginal revenue curve can always be found as the derivative of the total revenue function.

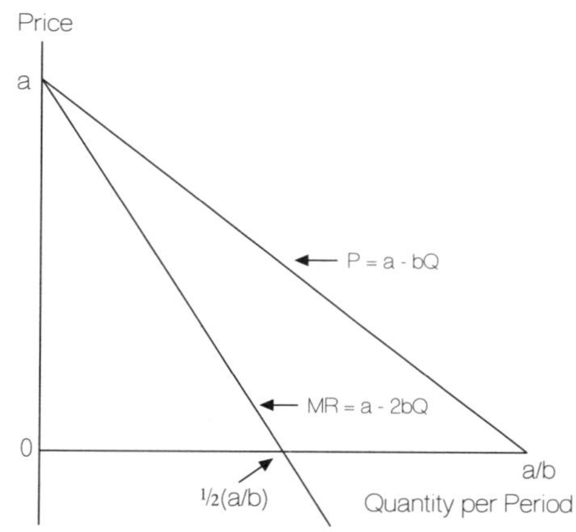

Figure 4-1
Linear demand and marginal revenue.

Suppose the demand curve is nonlinear, with the specific form shown in Equation 4-6:

$$Q = 100P^{-2} \tag{4-6}$$

This is an example of a general form $Q = aP^{-\eta}$ library, where the function has a constant price elasticity of demand equal to the exponent η. Thus the price elasticity of demand for Equation 4-6 is 2 everywhere. To find the marginal revenue curve for Equation 4-6, first solve for P:

$$P^2 = \frac{100}{Q}$$

so that

$$P = \frac{10}{\sqrt{Q}}$$

As Equation 4-7 shows, you multiply by Q to get the total revenue function:

$$R = 10Q^{\frac{1}{2}} \tag{4-7}$$

Finally, Equation 4-8 shows the result:

$$MR = \frac{dR}{dQ} = 5Q^{-\frac{1}{2}} \tag{4-8}$$

Figure 4-2 shows the demand curve (Equation 4-6) and the marginal revenue curve (Equation 4-8).

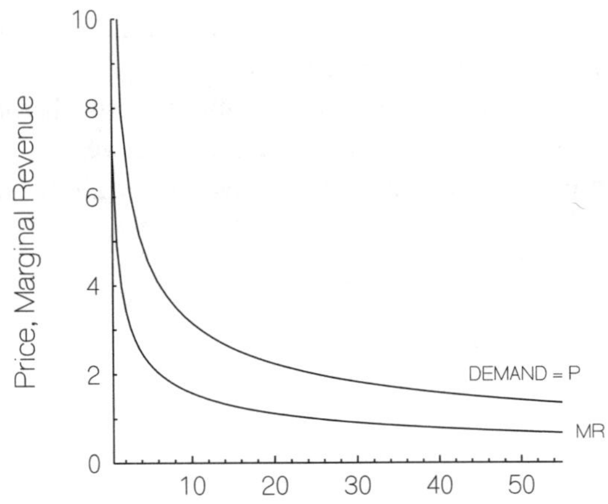

Figure 4-2
Nonlinear demand and marginal revenue.

4-1b Marginal Product

Chapter 2 introduced a short-run production function and derived its average product function. Now it is possible to find the marginal product schedule for the total product curve and examine the relationships between total, marginal, and average products. Equation 2-8 from Chapter 2, repeated here as Equation 4-9, specifies total product as a function of labor only:

$$TP = 12L^2 - L^3 \tag{4-9}$$

Marginal product is typically defined as the change in total product for a one-unit change in labor input. In other words, it is the slope of the total product curve, the derivative of total product:

$$MP = \frac{d(TP)}{dL} = 24L - 3L^2 \tag{4-10}$$

Figure 4-3 shows the relationship between total product, average product, and marginal product. Before the fourth unit of labor input, the *slope* of TP is increasing, meaning that MP must be increasing. A point of inflection occurs in TP where the labor input is four. As stated in Chapter 2, a point of inflection signals a change in concavity and, here, a change in the slope of TP from increasing to decreasing after four units of labor input. This means MP must be declining after L = 4. In the bottom section of the diagram, since MP increases until L = 4 and declines thereafter, the point above four units of labor input on the TP schedule must be where concavity changes.

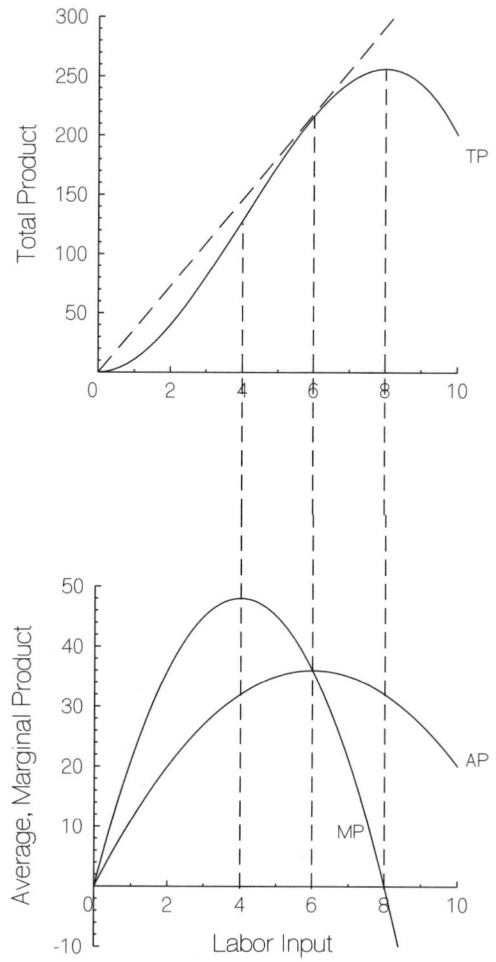

Figure 4-3
Total, average, and marginal product.

The diagram also reproduces the relationship between TP and AP. Specifically, average product is a maximum where a ray from the origin is tangent to the total product schedule. The student should be aware that in *any* marginal-average relationship, if the marginal exceeds the average, the average must be increasing, and if the marginal is less than the average, the average must be decreasing. The bottom half of the diagram shows this relationship clearly.

As a final point, the maximum of total product is found where marginal product is zero, since thereafter the additions to total product (marginal product) would be negative.

4-1c Marginal Utility

Much of the subject matter of microeconomics concerns utility analysis, where utility is a function of two—or more than two—commodities, as shown in Equation 4-11:

$$U = U(x,y) \tag{4-11}$$

where U is total utility and x and y are the amounts of good x and good y consumed. If a fixed level of utility is specified for the total utility function, the general equation would be transformed into an indifference curve. For each fixed level of utility there would be another indifference curve. The marginal utility of x is $\partial U/\partial x$, and the marginal utility of y is $\partial U/\partial y$.

The total differential of Equation 4-11 is shown in Equation 4-12:

$$dU = \frac{\partial U}{\partial x} dx + \frac{\partial U}{\partial y} dy \tag{4-12}$$

which is a general statement that the change in total utility (dU) is equal to the marginal utility of x times the change in x plus the marginal utility of y times the change in y. Along any single indifference curve, as more of one good and less of the other is consumed, total utility is constant; thus the change in utility, dU = 0. Setting dU = 0 in Equation 4-11 yields this result:

$$\frac{\partial U}{\partial y} dy = -\frac{\partial U}{\partial x} dx$$

Thus, Equation 4-13:

$$\frac{dy}{dx} = -\frac{\frac{\partial U}{\partial x}}{\frac{\partial U}{\partial y}} \tag{4-13}$$

Equation 4-10 shows that the slope of an indifference curve (dy/dx), also known as the *marginal rate of substitution of x for y*, is equal to (minus) the ratio of the marginal utility of x to the marginal utility of y. Order matters here, since the marginal rate of substitution of y for x is equal to the marginal utility of y divided by the marginal utility of x.

4-1d Marginal Cost

Economists often model short-run total cost functions (and sometimes long-run total cost functions) as cubic functions based on Equation 4-14:

$$TC = aQ^3 + bQ^2 + cQ + d \tag{4-14}$$

This form allows us to specify values for the parameters so that the corresponding marginal cost function has a decreasing section followed by an increasing section as output increases. The total cost function must therefore have a concave section followed by a convex section when viewed from below. Also, the total cost curve must have a positive slope everywhere, since more output means higher total costs. If the slope of total cost is positive everywhere, marginal cost cannot be negative. If we choose values such that $a > 0$, $b < 0$, $c > 0$, $d > 0$, and $b^2 < 3ac$, the desired shape of the total cost function will result. If you examine the restrictions on a, b, c, and d, you may be able to figure out why the sign restrictions are as they are. The last restriction, $b^2 < 3ac$, ensures that marginal cost is always positive.[1] The general equation for marginal cost based on Equation 4-14 is shown in Equation 4-15:

$$MC = \frac{d(TC)}{dQ} = 3aQ^2 + 2bQ + c \tag{4-15}$$

1. Marginal cost is a parabola when the total cost function is a cubic as described above. The marginal cost parabola must be U-shaped, so $a > 0$, and its minimum point must be at a positive value of cost. Chapter 5 covers methods for finding minimum points.

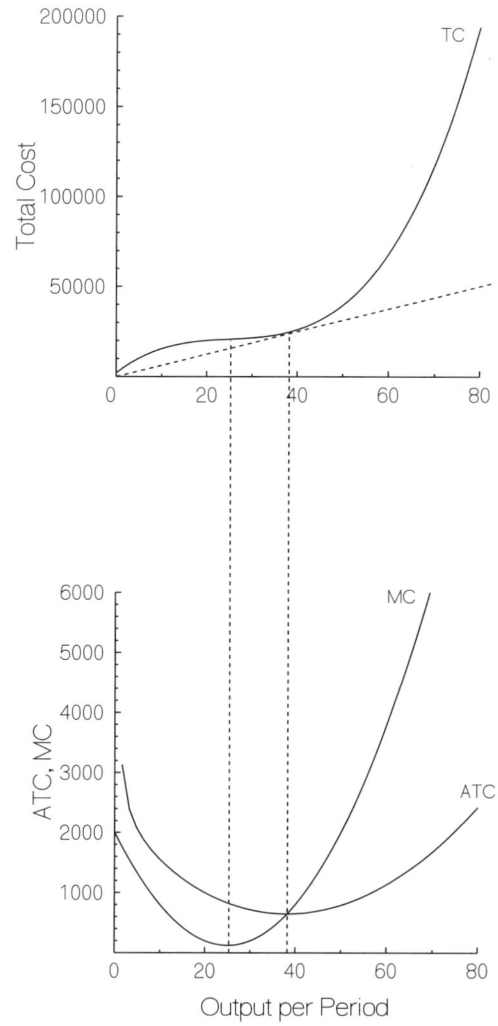

Figure 4-4
Total, average total, and marginal cost.

Consider the specific total cost function in Equation 4-16:

$$TC = Q^3 - 75Q^2 + 2000Q + 2000 \qquad (4\text{-}16)$$

This meets all of the restrictions above. The corresponding marginal cost function is shown in Equation 4-17:

$$MC = \frac{d(TC)}{dQ} = 3Q^2 - 150Q + 2000 \qquad (4\text{-}17)$$

Finally, the average (total) cost function, TC/Q, is as shown in Equation 4-18:

$$ATC = Q^2 - 75Q + 2000 + 2000/Q \qquad (4\text{-}18)$$

These functions are graphed in Figure 4-5. Notice that TC has an inflection point at an output of 25 units, which corresponds to the minimum point on marginal cost. Also, marginal cost is positive everywhere, since total cost has a positive slope everywhere. Finally, MC intersects ATC at the minimum of ATC. These are the general relationships that will hold for most short-run cost functions. There would also exist an average *variable* cost function as well, which would lie below

ATC and also be intersected at its minimum by marginal cost. (This function is not included in Figure 4-5 for simplicity.) The equation for AVC is found by subtracting fixed cost from total cost and then dividing by output. Fixed cost is the level of cost where output is zero (Q = 0), or $2000. Subtract 2000 from Equation 4-16 and divide the result by Q to obtain Equation 4-19:

$$AVC = Q^2 - 75Q + 2000 \quad (4\text{-}19)$$

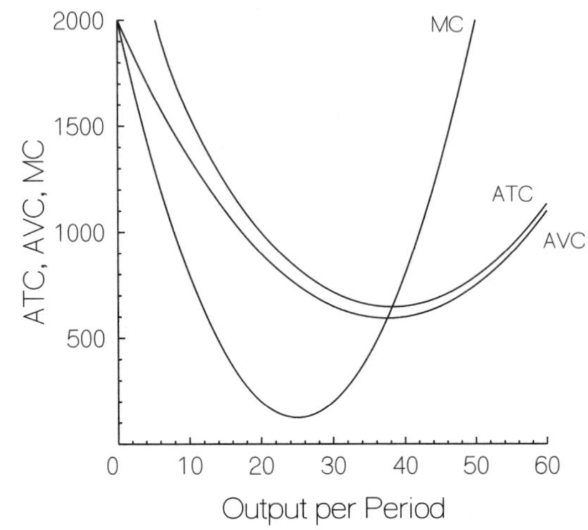

Figure 4-5
Average and marginal costs.

The difference between average total cost and average variable cost is average fixed cost. In this example, that difference is 2000/Q; therefore, as Q increases, the difference between the curves diminishes as shown in Figure 4-5, where the x and y scales have been expanded to show both average total and average variable cost.

Still other applications exist of the derivative as the marginal function to a total function. Marginal revenue product, the marginal rate of technical substitution, and marginal rates of taxation are examples. In each case, the principles presented here apply: If the total function is known, its derivative is the marginal function. If the average function is known, that function is multiplied by the proper independent variable to find the total function before taking the derivative to find the marginal relationship.

4-2 Elasticity and Total Expenditure

The student of microeconomics should already know the relationship between total expenditure and price elasticity of demand. Early in principles and intermediate micro it is usually *asserted* that if the coefficient of price elasticity is less than 1, price and total expenditure move in the same direction; if price falls, total expenditure falls; and if price rises, total expenditure rises. If the coefficient exceeds 1, price and total expenditure move in opposite directions. Knowledge of derivatives allows us to prove this proposition very simply. Total expenditure (TE) equals price times quantity (PQ), TE = PQ. Differentiating TE with respect to P by applying the product rule yields the following:

$$\frac{d(TE)}{dP} = P\frac{dQ}{dP} + Q\frac{dP}{dP}$$

and

$$\frac{d(TE)}{dP} = Q + P\frac{dQ}{dP}$$

$$\frac{d(TE)}{dP} = Q(1 + \frac{P}{Q}\frac{dQ}{dP})$$

and finally Equation 4-20:

$$\frac{d(TE)}{dP} = Q(1 - \eta) \qquad (4\text{-}20)$$

Since Q is always positive, the sign of d(TE)/dP depends only on whether η is greater or less than 1. If η is greater than 1, d(TE)/dP is negative, meaning that price and total expenditure move in opposite directions. If η is less than 1, d(TE)/dP is positive, meaning that price and total expenditure move in the same direction. Of course, when $\eta = 1$, d(TE)/dP = 0, so there would be no change in total expenditure if price were to change by a small amount.

4-3 Price, Marginal Revenue, and Elasticity

From the seller's point of view, the total expenditure in the previous section is total revenue. We already know (from section 4-1a) that the derivative of total revenue with respect to output is marginal revenue. Using this knowledge and the definition of price elasticity demand (see Equation 4-23 in the next section), we can now derive a valuable relationship between price (average revenue), marginal revenue, and price elasticity of demand. Recognizing that total expenditure on a good or the revenue (R) collected from sales of a good equals price times quantity (PQ), we have:

$$R = PQ$$

Differentiating with respect to Q to obtain marginal revenue gives us the following:

$$MR = \frac{dR}{dQ} = P\frac{dQ}{dQ} + Q\frac{dP}{dQ}$$

or

$$MR = P + Q\frac{dP}{dQ}$$

Now multiply the right-hand side by P/P so that we get this result

$$MR = \frac{P^2}{P} + \frac{PQ}{P}\frac{dP}{dQ}$$

and factoring yields this:

$$MR = P(1 + \frac{Q}{P}\frac{dP}{dQ})$$

The second term inside the parentheses is –1 times the reciprocal of price elasticity of demand (see the definition of price elasticity of demand). Then we can write Equation 4-21:

$$MR = P(1 - \frac{1}{\eta}) \qquad (4\text{-}21)$$

This definition is useful for several reasons. First, since P is always positive, MR is less than P, unless $\eta = \infty$, then P = MR. (When $\eta = \infty$ the demand curve is infinitely elastic or horizontal, as is the demand curve that the firm faces under the perfectly competitive model.) Second, the value of the price elasticity coefficient indicates whether marginal revenue is positive, negative, or zero. If $\eta > 1$, MR > 0; if $\eta < 1$, MR < 0; and if $\eta = 1$, MR = 0. Finally, if any two of P, MR, and η are known, the other can be found by substitution into Equation 4-21. For example, if MR = \$100 and P = \$200, Equation 4-21 can be solved for $\eta = 2$.

4-4 Elasticity and Nonlinear Demand Curves

Chapter 2 introduced a method for determining the price elasticity of linear demand curves. Linear demand curves are an expositional convenience; they are rarely found for real goods and services. When curves are nonlinear, the first derivative returns the slope of the function at any point, and the value of the slope can be used in computing the coefficient of price elasticity. Suppose a demand curve is given, as shown in Equation 4-22:

$$Q = 100 - 5P - P^2 \qquad (4\text{-}22)$$

where Q is quantity demanded and P is price in dollars. Written with the quantity demanded on the left-hand side, the derivative dQ/dP is one of the right-hand terms of the formula for elasticity, first presented in Chapter 2 as Equation 2-6 and repeated here as Equation 4-23:

$$\eta_d = -\frac{dQ}{dP} \bullet \frac{P}{Q} \qquad (4\text{-}23)$$

where $\Delta Q/\Delta P$ has been replaced by the derivative because we want to determine elasticity at a particular point. In this case, the derivative dQ/dP = –5 – 2P. Now suppose we want to measure elasticity at a price of, say, \$5. The quantity demanded must be 50 units, since $Q = 100 - 5(5) - 5^2 = 50$. The slope at this point is –15, since dQ/dP = –5 – 2(5) = –15. Then, using the formula for elasticity, we have the following result:

$$\eta_d = -(-15) \bullet \frac{5}{50} = 1.5$$

The price elasticity of demand can be computed for any other P, Q combination using Equation 4-23 and the derivative of Equation 4-22. Suppose the price is \$4. The quantity demanded from Equation 4-22 is 64 units, since $Q = 100 - 5(4) - 4^2 = 64$. The slope of the demand curve at this point is –13, since dQ/dP = –5 – 2(4) = –13. Substituting again into the elasticity formula:

$$\eta_d = -(-13) \bullet \frac{4}{64} = 0.8125$$

That is, the price elasticity of demand is 0.8125 at the point on the demand curve where P = 4 and Q = 64.

The student may have noticed that demand curves are often written with either P or Q on the left side. Suppose a demand equation is written with P on the left side and we want to determine the price elasticity for some P, Q combination. If the equation is simple enough, we can simply solve for Q, take the derivative, dQ/dP, substitute into Equation 4-23, and move on to the next problem. Suppose, however, that the demand equation is stated with P on the left side and the equation is more complicated, for example the version shown in Equation 4-24:

$$P = 1000 - .04Q^{3} - Q^{.5} \tag{4-24}$$

Solving for Q would be very difficult indeed. How can the derivative dQ/dP be found so that price elasticity can be computed? It turns out, for demand equations at least, that the derivative dP/dQ can be computed, and its *inverse*, 1/(dP/dQ), is, in fact, dQ/dP, which is what is needed to find η_d.

This procedure is sometimes stated as a separate rule for derivatives, the *inverse function rule*, and its use is dependent on the original function being *monotonic*. A function is monotonically increasing if successive increases in the independent variable (x) *always* lead to successive increases in the dependent variable, f(x). A function is monotonically decreasing if successive increases in the independent variable (x) *always* lead to successive decreases in the dependent variable, f(x). We know that market demand curves slope downward throughout, so demand curves are monotonically decreasing. This fact will allow us to find the price elasticity of demand for Equation 4-24 with relative ease.

First, differentiate Equation 4-24 with respect to Q:

$$\frac{dP}{dQ} = -.12Q^{2} - .5Q^{-.}$$

and since

$$\frac{1}{dP/dQ} = \frac{dQ}{dP}$$

The result is Equation 4-25:

$$\frac{dQ}{dP} = \frac{1}{-.12Q^{2} - .5Q^{-.5}} \tag{4-25}$$

The rest is arithmetic. Supposing Q = 25 in Equation 4-24, verify that P = 370. Substitute Q = 25 into Equation 4-25 to obtain this result:

$$\frac{dQ}{dP} = \frac{1}{-.12(25)^{2} - .5(1/\sqrt{25})} = -0.0133$$

Finally,

$$\eta_d = -(-0.0133) \cdot \frac{370}{25} = 0.197$$

In general, once the formula for the demand equation is known, the price elasticity of demand can be computed at a given point by substituting the P, Q combination and the derivative evaluated at that point into Equation 4-23.

4-5 A Digression on Homogeneous Equations

Some of the most important applications of derivatives and the marginal concept involve homogeneous equations. Suppose a certain economic relationship exists where z = f(x,y). If both x and y are changed by a fixed proportion, the function z may increase (or decrease) by the same proportion, a greater proportion, or a lesser proportion. If the function changes by the same proportion as x and y, the function is said to be *linearly homogeneous*[2] or homogeneous of degree one. In functional notation, the linearly homogeneous case is:

$$f(hx, hy) = hf(x,y) = hz$$

where h is some constant.

The *linearly* homogeneous function is a special case of a more general relationship for homogeneous functions. A function is homogeneous of degree r if, when each of the independent variables is multiplied by a constant h, the value of the function changes by h^r. For two independent variables, the general functional result would be as shown in Equation 4-26:

$$f(hx, hy) = h^r f(x,y) = h^r z \tag{4-26}$$

If r = 1, the function is *linearly homogeneous*, as above. If r = 0, the function is homogeneous of degree zero, and there would be no change at all in the function for any fixed proportionate change in each of the independent variables, since $h^0 = 1$. If r exceeds 1, say r = 2, the function is homogeneous of degree two, and the proportion by which the function changes is twice the proportion by which the independent variables change.

Examples

1. *If* $z = f(x, y) = x/y$, *then*

$$f(hx, hy) = hx/hy = x/y = h^0(x/y)$$

So z is homogeneous of degree zero.

2. *If* $z = f(x, y) = 3x + 2y$, *then*

$$f(hx, hy) = 3hx + 2hy$$
$$= h(3x + 2y)$$

So z is homogeneous of degree one, or linearly homogeneous.

3. *If* $z = f(x,y) = y^2x$, *then*

$$f(hx, hy) = (hy)^2hx = h^2y^2hx$$
$$= h^3(y^2x)$$

2. This in no way implies that the function is linear.

So z is homogeneous of degree three.

4. If $z = f(x,y) = y^{\alpha}x^{\beta}$, then

$$f(hx, hy) = (hy)^{\alpha}(hx)^{\beta} = h^{\alpha}y^{\alpha}h^{\beta}x^{\beta}$$
$$= h^{\alpha+\beta}(y^{\alpha}x^{\beta})$$

So z is homogeneous of degree $\alpha + \beta$.

4-5a The Cobb-Douglas Production Function

The equation presented in example 4 above is a form of the Cobb-Douglas production function,[3] which is often used to represent production relationships and other relationships such as utility functions and even demand functions. This function was presented at the end of Chapter 1 as an example of a function of more than one variable. A typical representation for the Cobb-Douglas production function is the form shown in Equation 4-27:

$$Q = AL^{\alpha}K^{1-\alpha} \qquad (4\text{-}27)$$

where $0 < \alpha < 1$ and A is a positive constant. Since the exponents sum to 1, $\alpha + (1 - \alpha) = 1$, the function is linearly homogeneous. To prove, multiply both inputs by h:

$$Q = A(hL)^{\alpha}(hK)^{1-\alpha} = Ah^{\alpha}L^{\alpha}h^{1-a}K^{1-a}$$
$$= h(AL^{\alpha}K^{1-a})$$

The economic meaning of this result is that the linearly homogeneous Cobb-Douglas production function is subject to *constant returns to scale.* That is, if the inputs are both increased by an equal given proportion, output will increase by that same proportion.

The Cobb-Douglas production function need not be linearly homogeneous. If the function is written without the restriction that the exponents must sum to one, you get Equation 4-28:

$$Q = AL^{\alpha}K^{\beta} \qquad (4\text{-}28)$$

Statistical methods can be employed to estimate the parameters A, α, and β. Then, if $\alpha + \beta = 1$, the production function exhibits constant returns to scale. But if $\alpha + \beta > 1$, increasing returns to scale are implied, and if $\alpha + \beta < 1$, the production function is subject to decreasing returns to scale.

4-5b Properties of Linearly Homogeneous Production Functions

The Cobb-Douglas production function is not the only representation of a linearly homogeneous production function. A number of important properties apply to *all* linearly homogeneous production functions, including the Cobb-Douglas formulation. These properties are demonstrated for the Cobb-Douglas formulation in this section, since it is used so often in the study of microeconomics.

Property I *The marginal products of each input depend only on the ratio of capital to labor (or whatever inputs are specified) and not on the levels of those inputs.* Stated simply, if K = 100 and L = 50, the capital-to-labor ratio is 2, and if K = 500 and L = 250, the capital-to-labor ratio is also 2. If the marginal product of labor is

3. Douglas, P.H., *Theory of Wages.* New York: Macmillan Company, 1934.

50 bags of potato chips when K = 100 and L = 50, then, when K = 500 and L = 250, the marginal product of labor is still 50 bags of potato chips. To prove, differentiate Equation 4-27 with respect to L to obtain the marginal product of labor shown in Equations 4-29 and 4-29′:

$$\frac{\partial Q}{\partial L} = \alpha A L^{\alpha - 1} K^{1-\alpha} \tag{4-29}$$

$$\frac{\partial Q}{\partial L} = \alpha A \left(\frac{K^{1-\alpha}}{L^{1-\alpha}} \right) = \alpha A \left(\frac{K}{L} \right)^{1-\alpha} \tag{4-29′}$$

Since A and α are both constants, the marginal product of labor depends only on the capital-to-labor ratio (K/L); as the ratio of capital to labor increases, the marginal product of labor rises. Similarly, differentiate Equation 4-27 with respect to K to obtain the marginal product of capital, as in Equations 4-30 and 4-30′:

$$\frac{\partial Q}{\partial K} = (1 - \alpha) A L^{\alpha} K^{1-\alpha-1} \tag{4-30}$$

$$\frac{\partial Q}{\partial K} = (1 - \alpha) A \left(\frac{K^{-\alpha}}{L^{-\alpha}} \right) = (1 - \alpha) A \left(\frac{K}{L} \right)^{-\alpha} \tag{4-30′}$$

The marginal product of capital also depends on only the capital-to-labor ratio. As the ratio of capital to labor increases, the marginal product of capital *decreases.* Alternatively, as the labor-to-capital ratio increases, the marginal product of capital increases. Notice that the exponent attached to the capital-to-labor ratio in Equation 4-30′ is $-\alpha$, which means that the marginal product of capital may also be written this way:

$$\frac{\partial Q}{\partial K} = (1 - \alpha) A \left(\frac{L}{K} \right)^{\alpha}$$

Property II *The average products of each input depend only on the ratio of capital to labor (or whatever inputs are specified) and not on the levels of those inputs.* To prove, simply divide both sides of Equation 4-27 by L to obtain the average product of labor, and by K to obtain the average product of capital (see Equations 4-31 and 4-32):

$$\frac{Q}{L} = A \left(\frac{K}{L} \right)^{1-\alpha} \tag{4-31}$$

$$\frac{Q}{K} = A \left(\frac{K}{L} \right)^{-\alpha} = A \left(\frac{L}{K} \right)^{\alpha} \tag{4-32}$$

Equations 4-31 and 4-32, the average products of labor and capital respectively, are both functions of the capital-to-labor ratio alone.

Property III *The sum of the marginal product of labor times the level of labor input and the marginal product of capital times the level of capital input will be identical to the level of output.* See Equation 4-33.

$$Q \equiv L\frac{\partial Q}{\partial L} + K\frac{\partial Q}{\partial K} \qquad (4\text{-}33)$$

This result is an application of Euler's Theorem,[4] named after Swiss mathematician Leonhard Euler[5] (1707–83). This result is easily demonstrated for the Cobb-Douglas production function. Using the marginal products from Equations 4-29 and 4-30 and substituting into Equation 4-33, we have the result shown in Equation 4-34:

$$Q = \alpha AL^{\alpha-1}K^{1-\alpha}(L) + (1-\alpha)AL^{\alpha}K^{-\alpha}(K)$$
$$Q = \alpha AL^{\alpha}K^{1-\alpha} + (1-\alpha)AL^{\alpha}K^{1-\alpha} = AL^{\alpha}K^{1-\alpha} \qquad (4\text{-}34)$$

Since this result holds for any values of L and K, Euler's Theorem may be expressed as an identity in Equation 4-33.

Euler's Theorem has implications for income distribution theory. Consider Equation 4-33. If each factor is paid an amount equal to its marginal product, the sum of the totals paid to each factor (marginal product of labor times the level of labor *plus* marginal product of capital times the level of capital) will exhaust total output (Q). In other words, nothing will be left over for economic profit; economic profit is zero. This is, of course, the long-run condition for a competitive industry. But do not assume that a linearly homogeneous production function is a necessary precondition to zero economic profit; zero profit is due to entry and exit of firms in the given industry. Also, factors will not necessarily be paid their marginal products when competition in the input market is imperfect.

Property IV *The exponent of a variable input is the (partial) elasticity of output with respect to that variable for the Cobb-Douglas production function.*

While the first three properties apply to all linearly homogeneous production functions, this property applies specifically to the Cobb-Douglas formulation. Suppose that in Equation 4-27, $\alpha = .75$. Then the elasticity of output with respect to labor is .75, and since $1 - \alpha = .25$, the elasticity of output with respect to capital is .25. To show this result, define the elasticity of output with respect to labor as the percentage change in output divided by the percentage change in labor input, as in Equation 4-35:

$$\eta_{QL} = \frac{\partial Q/Q}{\partial L/L} = \frac{\partial Q}{\partial L}\cdot\frac{L}{Q} \qquad (4\text{-}35)$$

4. For a proof of Euler's Theorem, see D. Wade Hands, *Introductory Mathematical Economics.* Lexington, Massachusetts: D.C. Heath and Company, 1991, p. 97.

5. Euler is pronounced "oiler," as in "Houston Oiler," for you old Texas football fans. So call him Leonhard "Houston" Euler, with apologies to Chris "Boomer" Berman.

Using the marginal product of labor from Equation 4-29, we have the following:

$$\eta_{QL} = \frac{\alpha A L^{\alpha-1} K^{1-\alpha} L}{Q}$$

$$\eta_{QL} = \frac{\alpha A L^{\alpha} K^{1-\alpha}}{A L^{\alpha} K^{1-\alpha}} = \alpha \tag{4-36}$$

A similar derivation verifies that the elasticity of output with respect to capital (η_{QK}) is equal to $1 - \alpha$ or, more generally, β, as in Equation 4-28, if the exponent of capital is not restricted to $1 - \alpha$.

Property V *The exponent of each variable input represents the relative income share of that factor in total product (Q) for a linearly homogeneous Cobb-Douglas production function.*

The proof of this proposition is precisely that offered in Equation 4-36; when labor is paid its marginal product, the total payment to labor is $MP_L \cdot L$ and labor's share is $MP_L \cdot L/Q$, which equals α. Why, then, must the function be linearly homogeneous for this property to hold as stated in the definition? This is because the "shares" do not sum to 1 according to Euler's Theorem unless the function is linearly homogeneous. Indeed, a modified version of Euler's Theorem would state that the sum of the factor payments would equal rQ, where r is the degree of homogeneity, as in Equation 4-37:

$$rQ \equiv L\frac{\partial Q}{\partial L} + K\frac{\partial Q}{\partial K} \tag{4-37}$$

If $r > 1$, the payments to the factors would exceed total product (Q), and if $r < 1$, the payments to the factors would be less than total product. In either case, the value of the exponent would not by itself equal the "share" of total product paid to that factor.

Other Properties

There are still other characteristics of the linearly homogeneous production functions and the Cobb-Douglas formulation, as shown in the following list:

- The marginal rate of technical substitution is the same for every isoquant where it intersects a ray (straight line) drawn through the origin.
- The expansion path for differing (higher) levels of expenditure on inputs is linear.
- The ridge lines are linear.

Suffice it to say that linearly homogeneous production functions are an important class of production functions for both theoretical and empirical work, and the Cobb-Douglas specific form has some unique mathematical properties that make it an important tool for the study of microeconomics.

4-5c Demand Functions Homogeneous of Degree Zero

Another application of homogeneous equations centers on demand theory. Often demand equations are specified that are *homogeneous of degree zero in prices and income.* These demand functions have tremendous theoretical appeal and are in fact implied by the budget constraints typically presented in microeconomics.

With a given utility function, if all prices and income were to change in the same proportion (for example, income and all prices double), the budget line would be unchanged, and therefore the amounts of the goods consumed would remain the same. These conditions are often referred to as the *absence of money illusion.*

One specification of a demand equation that is homogeneous of degree zero is a logical extension of the type of equations presented at the beginning of this section. Suppose Patrick Lowry spends his entire allowance on tacos and burritos and, further, that the specific form of his demand curve for tacos is as shown in Equation 4-38:

$$Q_T = 100P_T^{-1.8}P_B^{1.1}Y^{0.7} \quad (4\text{-}38)$$

where Q_T is the quantity of tacos demanded, P_T is the price of tacos, P_B is the price of burritos, and Y is income. Note that the exponents, –1.8, 1.1, and 0.7, sum to zero. With this multiplicative form, the fact that the exponents sum to zero means that the demand equation is homogeneous of degree zero in prices and income. Additionally, the exponents are elasticities of demand with respect to the variable to which they are attached. (Note that the elasticity with respect to P_T is –1 times the exponent, so $\eta = 1.8$ for our definition of η.)

The price elasticity of demand for Equation 4-38 would be defined as shown in Equation 4-39:

$$\eta_T = -\frac{\partial Q_T}{\partial P_T} \cdot \frac{P_T}{Q_T} \quad (4\text{-}39)$$

First, compute the partial derivative of Q_T with respect to P_T:

$$\frac{\partial Q_T}{\partial P_T} = -180P_T^{-2.8}P_B^{1.1}Y^{0.7}$$

Then multiply by –1 and by P_T and divide by the right-hand definition of Q_T in Equation 4-38:

$$\eta_T = -\frac{\partial Q_T}{\partial P_T} \cdot \frac{P_T}{Q_T} = \frac{180P_T^{-2.8}P_B^{1.1}Y^{0.7}(P_T)}{100P_T^{-1.8}P_B^{1.1}Y^{0.7}} = \frac{180}{100} = 1.8$$

The cross-price elasticity between tacos and the price of burritos, η_{TB}, is defined by Equation 4-40:

$$\eta_{TB} = \frac{\partial Q_T}{\partial P_B} \cdot \frac{P_B}{Q_T} \quad (4\text{-}40)$$

which will return the percentage change in the quantity of tacos demanded for a 1% change in the price of burritos. Notice that the negative sign is not present as in Equation 4-39, so that the sign of η_{TB} (or the partial derivative, $\partial Q_T/\partial P_B$) will indicate whether the goods are complements or substitutes. If η_{TB} is positive, the goods are substitutes, since a rise in the price of burritos would cause a rise in the quantity of tacos demanded. If η_{TB} is negative, the goods are complements, since a rise in the price of burritos would cause the quantity demanded to fall for tacos.

To compute η_{TB}, take the partial derivative of the demand function (Equation 4-38) with respect to P_B:

$$\frac{\partial Q_T}{\partial P_B} = 110P_T^{-1.8}P_B^{0.1}Y^{0.7}$$

Then multiply by P_B and divide by the right-hand definition of Q_T:

$$\eta_{TB} = \frac{\partial Q_T}{\partial P_B} \cdot \frac{P_B}{Q_T} = \frac{110P_T^{-1.8}P_B^{0.1}Y^{0.7}(P_B)}{100P_T^{-1.8}P_B^{1.1}Y^{0.7}} = \frac{110}{100} = 1.1$$

By a similar procedure, the income elasticity of demand (η_Y) can be computed and is equal to the exponent 0.7.

Now suppose that all prices and incomes rise by 10%. Since the demand equation is homogeneous of degree zero in prices and income, the quantity of tacos demanded should remain the same. The arithmetic is as follows:

1. The rise in the price of tacos causes quantity demanded to fall by 18% = –(1.8)(10%).[6]
2. The rise in the price of burritos causes quantity demanded to rise by 11% = (1.1)(10%).
3. The rise in income causes the quantity demanded to rise by 7% = (0.7)(10%). The 18% fall is exactly offset by an 18% rise (11%) + (7%).

4-6 Summary

The applications of the concept of a derivative in this chapter allow us to compute marginal functions and elasticity coefficients, and investigate certain production and demand specifications. All of these are important to our understanding of microeconomic principles. The next application of the derivative lies in its use in finding maxima and minima for economic relationships. Without mastery of maximization and minimization techniques, much of the subject matter of microeconomics will be beyond our grasp.

Problems

1. Suppose the total cost of producing potato chips can be approximated by the following function:

   $$TC = 10q^3 + 160$$

   where TC is total costs in dollars and q is hundreds of bags per week.

   (a) Calculate the marginal cost function.
   (b) Write the equation for the average total cost (ATC) function.
   (c) Find the output (in hundreds of bags of potato chips) where marginal cost is equal to average total cost. At this output, average total cost is at its minimum value. Explain why.
   (d) At the output in part (c), what is the average total cost per bag of chips?

6. Here we must remember that the quantity demanded of a good and its own price move in opposite directions, hence the negative sign. If price elasticity were not defined with a negative sign in front (which makes the measure positive), the additional negative sign here would be unnecessary.

2. You will need a calculator for this one. The output of Rock-Flight golf balls can be modeled as a Cobb-Douglas production function of the following form:

$$Q = 10L^{.75}K^{.25}$$

where Q = output in dozens of balls per month, L = labor input, and K = capital input.

(a) Calculate the marginal product of labor.
(b) Calculate the marginal product of capital.
(c) Find the average products of labor and capital.
(d) If K = 50 and L = 80, how many dozen Rock-Flights will be produced in this month? Find the answer by first substituting into the production function, ($Q = 10L^{.75}K^{.25}$) and then by using the marginal products you computed in parts (a) and (b) to this question and applying Euler's Theorem.

3. Again refer to the production function in Problem 2 concerning the golf balls.

(a) Is the production function linearly homogeneous? Explain how you know.
(b) Examine the marginal product and average product functions you calculated in Problem 2. Are these homogeneous equations? If so, of what degree? What is the *economic* interpretation of your answer?

4. The production of paperback textbooks is characterized by a Cobb-Douglas production function of this form:

$$Q = 20L^{.4}K^{.5}$$

where Q is the output in books per year, L is labor input, and K is capital input.

(a) What is the degree of homogeneity of the production function?
(b) Calculate the marginal product of labor.
(c) Calculate the marginal product of capital.
(d) Find the level of output for K = 20 and L = 30.
(e) Now find the total factor payment by computing $MP_L \cdot L + MP_K \cdot K$. Show, numerically, that this is the same answer that could have been computed from Equation 4-37, the modified version of Euler's Theorem, that is rQ, where r is the degree of homogeneity.

5. A utility function is given by the following equation:

$$U = x + 2x^{.5}y^{.5} + y$$

We are interested in finding the marginal rate of substitution of x for y ($MRS_{x \text{ for } y}$). If y is on the vertical axis and x is on the horizontal axis in an indifference map, the $MRS_{x \text{ for } y}$ is –1 times the slope of an indifference curve; in other words, –dy/dx.

(a) Treat U as an implicit function with a specific level of utility, meaning that the left side of the utility function is a constant. Differentiate the function implicitly and "solve" for dy/dx. The MRS is then –dy/dx.

(b) The marginal rate of substitution of x for y is also equal to the marginal utility of x (MU_x) divided by the marginal utility of y (MU_y). Partially differentiate the utility function with respect to x to obtain the marginal utility of x, and do the same with respect to y to obtain the marginal utility of y. Now form the ratio MU_x/MU_y. Check that your answer agrees with part (a).

(c) Compute the total differential of U (dU), set dU = 0, and "solve" for dy/dx. As you can see, there are a number of ways to get the same result.

6. Consider the following demand curve:

$$P = \frac{10 - 2P}{Q}$$

Find the coefficient of price elasticity of demand where Q = 3 by:

(a) Solving the equation for Q, calculating dQ/dP, and applying Equation 4-23 from this chapter.

(b) Finding the marginal revenue function and solving Equation 4-21 for η.

7. Given the following demand curve:

$$Q = 10P^{-2}$$

prove that the coefficient of price elasticity of demand is 2 everywhere.

8. Now that you have finished with Problem 7, let's do it again! This time, follow the rules of logarithms to take the natural log of each side of $Q = 10P^{-2}$. Now differentiate both sides of this result with respect to P (the left side should be 1/Q = dQ/dP). Multiply both sides of the equation by –P. You should now have the definition for price elasticity of demand on the left side and the number 2 on the right side.

Assuming that you have answered this problem correctly, you have just proven a general result. The definition on the left side is the derivative of ln Q with respect to P (d(ln Q)/dP), divided by the derivative of ln P with respect to P, all multiplied by –1. Stated differently, if we differentiate ln Q with respect to ln P, rather than P, and multiply by –1, the result will be the elasticity coefficient. Written generally, if

$$Q = aP^{-\eta}$$

and therefore

$$\ln Q = \ln a - \eta \ln P$$

then

$$-\frac{d(\ln Q)}{d(\ln P)} = \eta$$

9. The Checkers Pizza Delivery Company finds its quarterly sales to be given by this function:

$$S = 20e^{.15t}$$

where S is in thousands of pies per quarter, e = 2.71828..., the base of the natural logarithms, and t is the number of quarters since the firm began doing business.

(a) The quarterly (instantaneous) rate of growth of sales is the change in sales with respect to time (quarters) divided by the level of sales; that is, (dS/dt)/S. Prove that (dS/dt)/S is equal to .15 or 15%.
(b) More generally, if the formula is $S = Ae^{rt}$, where A and r are given constants and S, t, and e are as before, prove that the quarterly rate of growth equals r.
(c) Find sales in the fifth quarter (t = 5) since the firm's start-up.

10. The monthly short-run total cost of producing aluminum baseball bats can be approximated by the following exponential function:

$$TC = 100e^{.2q}$$

where TC is cost in thousands of dollars, q is thousands of bats per month, and e is the base of the natural logarithms.

(a) Calculate marginal cost.
(b) Write the expression for average total cost.
(c) How much is fixed cost?
(d) Show that average total cost equals marginal cost at the output q = 5, and explain why this the minimum for average total cost.
(e) More generally, show that if the cost function is given by $TC = Ae^{bq}$, where A and b are positive constants and e and q are as before, the minimum of average total cost occurs at the output 1/b.

Chapter 5

Maximization and Minimization

Maximization and minimization are central to microeconomic theory. Individuals are assumed to maximize utility. Firms are assumed to maximize profit. The firm, under the model of perfect competition, operates at the minimum of average cost in the long run. Additionally, most of these models of maximization and minimization activities are undertaken with one or more constraints on the choices; consumer choice is constrained by the level of income, and college students allocate their time to studying economics in competition with other activities and the constraint of time.

This chapter begins by introducing the general theory of maximization and minimization of functions of one variable. The argument is then extended to functions of more than one variable and functions that are subject to one or more constraints. The techniques covered in this chapter are used extensively in microeconomic analysis. Gaining an understanding of these techniques should enhance the student's understanding of the mathematical treatment of maximization and minimization and the economic meaning of the techniques in application.

Outline

5-1 A Simple Maximization Problem

In teaching microeconomic theory, I always ask my students how to find the maximum (or minimum) point of some simple well-behaved function that has such a point. Typically, about half of the class has never taken calculus, or their instruction in calculus was so long ago that they do not know where to start. Students with a recent knowledge of calculus can usually be prodded into saying ". . . take the derivative and set it equal to zero." However, if I then ask why this technique will allow us to find the extreme point (maximum or minimum), even current calculus students often cannot provide a satisfactory explanation. For these reasons, we will begin this chapter with a simple intuitive introduction of how and why we can use calculus to find maximum and minimum values.

Suppose we have a function relating profit to output of the form shown in Equation 5-1:

$$y = 6x - x^2 \tag{5-1}$$

where we assume that y is profit in thousands of dollars per week, and x is output in thousands of tons of coal per week. We want to find the output at which profit is maximized, and the level of maximum profit. Figure 5-1 contains the graph of the profit function. The graph allows us to answer our final questions immediately, so by graphing the equation we have read the last page in the murder mystery to find out who did the crime, without the fun of reading the plot. It is clear from the graph that profit, along the y-axis, reaches a maximum at an output rate of three tons per week, and the level of profit is $9,000 dollars per week. As you have probably guessed, it is not always this easy.

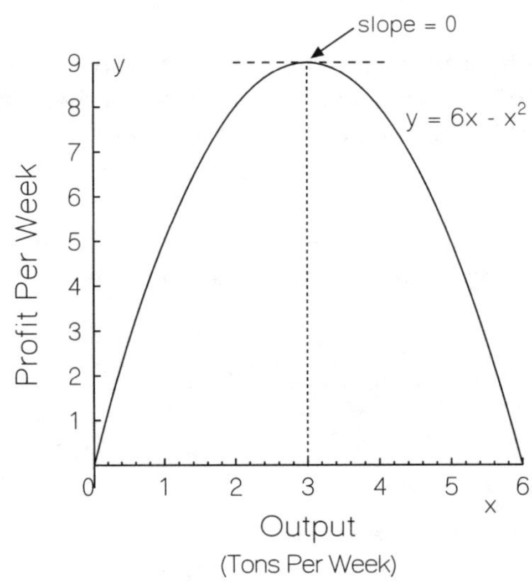

Figure 5-1
Profit as a function of output.

What we want to understand is how to use calculus to find these points, so that when the results are not so obvious we will still be able to solve the problem. To begin, what can we say about the point on the curve where x = 3 and y = 9? That is, what distinguishes that point from all other points, and how does this characteristic allow us to identify this position as a maximum? To answer, closely examine the slope of the function as x increases from 0 to 3. Over this range, the slope of $y = 6x - x^2$ is positive but decreasing. After x = 3, as x increases, the slope is negative and becoming steeper. This analysis suggests two conclusions:

- The function, $y = f(x) = 6x - x^2$, has reached some sort of maximum at $x = 3$.
- At the point on the curve where $x = 3$, the slope is zero. In the diagram, a tangent to the curve is drawn at the maximum point and its slope (and therefore the slope of the function) is zero. No other tangent to the curve will have a slope of zero.

These two conclusions are the foundation for using our knowledge of calculus to find the maximum (and minimum) points for a wide variety of applications. We already know that the derivative of a function is the slope of that function. Also, we know that for a well-behaved function[1] such as $y = 6x - x^2$, the slope of the function will be zero at a maximum (or a minimum).[2] Then it follows that if we can find the derivative (slope) of the function and find the value for x at which the derivative is zero, this value of x, when substituted into the original or primitive function, will return the maximum (or minimum) value for $y = f(x)$.

Although the answers are already known for this profit function, let's follow the steps outlined above. First, differentiate the profit function, $y = 6x - x^2$, in order to find its slope, as shown in Equation 5-2:

$$\frac{dy}{dx} = 6 - 2x \tag{5-2}$$

Second, set the derivative equal to zero and solve for x:

$$0 = 6 - 2x$$
$$2x = 6$$
$$x = 3$$

So the slope of the profit function is zero at $x = 3$. This means that the value of y in the profit function is a maximum when $x = 3$. The third step is to simply substitute $x = 3$ into the primitive function to find the maximum value of y (profit):

$$y_{max} = 6(3) - 3^2 = 9$$

Again, this was already evident from the graph in Figure 5-1.

Figure 5-2 provides a geometric explanation of the relationship between the derivative and the maximum value for the primitive function. The graph at top, panel A, is the profit function, $y = 6x - x^2$. The graph in the middle, panel B, is the derivative of the profit function, $dy/dx = y' = 6 - 2x$. Notice the relationship between the derivative and the profit function. Between $x = 0$ and $x = 3$, the slope of the profit function is positive; therefore, the value of the derivative (y') must be positive in panel B over the same range for x. To repeat, the derivative is the slope of the profit function and the graph of the derivative is above zero along the vertical axis for $x < 3$. For $x > 3$, the slope of the profit function is negative and therefore the value of the derivative in panel B is negative; that is, the graph of the derivative must lie below zero on the vertical axis for $x > 3$.

1. Section 5-3 discusses functions for which maximum and minimum values cannot be found by these techniques.
2. Methods for distinguishing between maximum and minimum values will be considered momentarily.

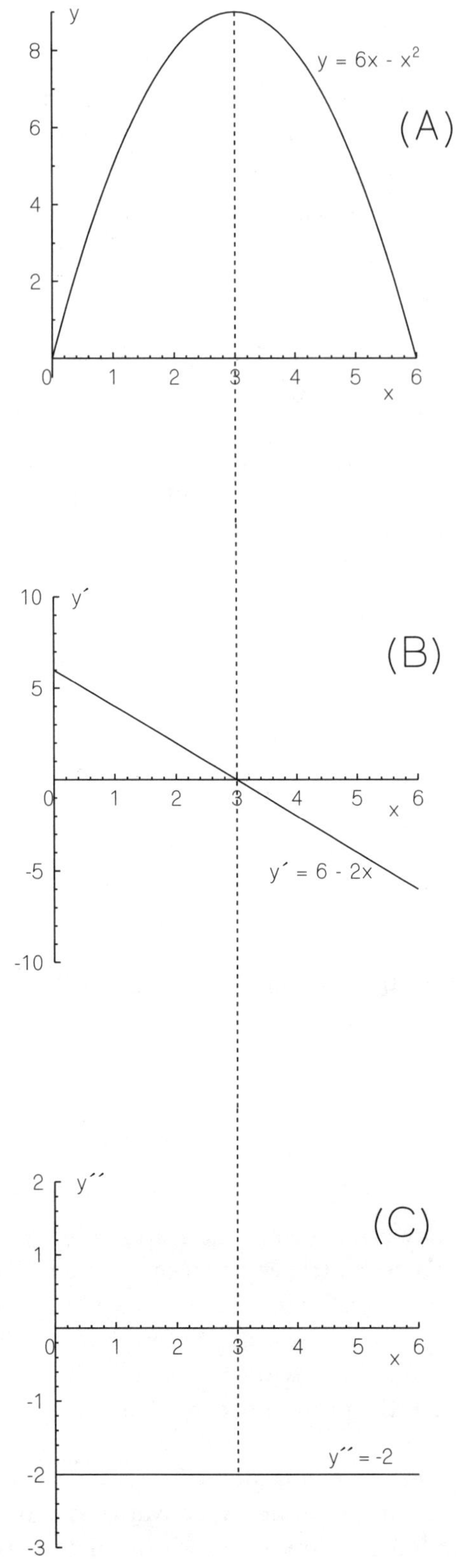

Figure 5-2
Maximization: a geometric interpretation.

Since the slope of the profit function is positive for $x < 3$ and negative for $x > 3$, the profit function must reach a maximum where $x = 3$. Only where the derivative is zero (crossing the x axis at $x = 3$) is the profit function at this maximum, and where the derivative is zero, the slope of the profit function must be zero.

As you may have noticed, there is another part to the graph in Figure 5-2; the final twist in the plot. The graph in panel C is the derivative of the derivative. The derivative of the derivative is typically called the second derivative, since it marks the second time a derivative has been found that is based on the original function. When this terminology is used, the derivative of the original function (in the middle panel) is called the first derivative. So, to compute a second derivative for a given primitive function, differentiate the function to obtain the first derivative, and then differentiate the first derivative to obtain the second derivative. Typical symbols for the second derivative are d^2y/dx^2 and y''.

What information does the second derivative provide? If the second derivative is negative at the value of x for which we have found the slope of the original function to be zero, then the value of the original function must be a maximum rather than a minimum. Why is this so? Again, examine Figure 5-2. In panel A, the slope of the original function is positive for values of $x < 3$ and negative for values of $x > 3$ (and, therefore, a maximum at $x = 3$). The value of the (first) derivative along the y axis in panel B must be positive for $x < 3$ and then become negative for $x > 3$. This can happen only if the derivative in panel B is negatively sloped. Finally, since the second derivative indicates the slope of the first derivative (in this case, the slope of y' must be negative), this proves that we have found a maximum for the original function.

Using the second derivative to determine whether the primitive function is a maximum or a minimum is known as the second derivative test. The same determination can be made by evaluating the first derivative below and above the value of x for $y' = 0$. If the derivative is positive below and negative above that value of x, a maximum exists for $y = f(x)$. If (as in the next section) the derivative is negative below and positive above that value of x where y' equals zero, a minimum exists for $y = f(x)$. This method is known as the first derivative test.

The second derivative has two additional interpretations relating to the original function:

- First, the sign of the second derivative at the value of x for which the first derivative is zero indicates the concavity of the original function. The profit function in panel A is concave downward or "bowed outward" from below. If the function were "U-shaped," like an average cost function, it would be called *concave upward* (or *convex from below*).

- Second, the second derivative is also the *rate of change* of the original function. If the first derivative is positive and the second derivative is negative, the original function is *increasing at a decreasing rate.* This is the case in Figure 5-2 for $0 < x < 3$. If the first derivative is negative and the second derivative is also negative, the function is *decreasing at an increasing rate.* This is the case in Figure 5-2 for $x > 3$. The other cases follow in logical fashion: If the first derivative is negative and the second derivative is positive, the original function is *decreasing at a decreasing rate* (see Figure 5-3 for $0 < x < 2$), and if the first derivative is positive and the second derivative is also positive, the original function is *increasing at an increasing rate* (see Figure 5-3 for $x > 2$).

The concavity of a function has important implications for distinguishing between a maximum and a minimum value. For a smooth function such as $y = 6x - x^2$, if the first derivative over some interval for x has a negative slope, the slope of the original function is decreasing. The original function must be concave downward, and since the first derivative has a negative slope over this interval, the second derivative must be negative over the same interval for x. If the second derivative is positive for some interval for x, the original or primitive function must be concave upward. The conclusions of this discussion are as follows:

- If $d^2y/dx^2 < 0$ over some interval for x, y = f(x) is concave downward on that interval.
- If $d^2y/dx^2 > 0$ over some interval for x, y = f(x) is concave upward on that interval.

Of course, if a function is concave downward and the slope of the function at x = a is zero, the value of the function at x = a is a maximum value. On the other hand, if a function is concave upward and the slope of the function at x = a is zero, the value of the function at x = a is a minimum value.

5-2 A Simple Minimization Problem

Suppose we have an equation for average cost as it relates to output, as shown in Equation 5-3:

$$y = x^2 - 4x + 6 \tag{5-3}$$

where y is average cost in thousands of dollars, and x is output, say thousands of motorcycles produced per year. The goal is to find the output at which average cost is at a minimum. Since this function is smooth, we should be able to use the procedures outlined in the previous section 5-1 to find the minimum value for y without trouble.

First, compute the first derivative for Equation 5-4:

$$\frac{dy}{dx} = 2x - 4 \tag{5-4}$$

Second, set the derivative equal to zero and solve for x:

$$0 = 2x - 4$$

$$2x = 4$$

$$x = 2$$

So the slope of the average cost function is zero at x = 2. This means that the value of y in the average cost function is a minimum when x = 2. The third step is simply to substitute x = 2 into the primitive function to find the minimum value of y (average cost):

$$y_{min} = 2^2 - 4(2) + 6 = 2$$

or $2,000 per motorcycle. The final step is to determine that this is in fact a minimum and not a maximum value for y. The second derivative provides the necessary information, as shown in Equation 5-5:

$$\frac{d^2y}{dx^2} = 2 \tag{5-5}$$

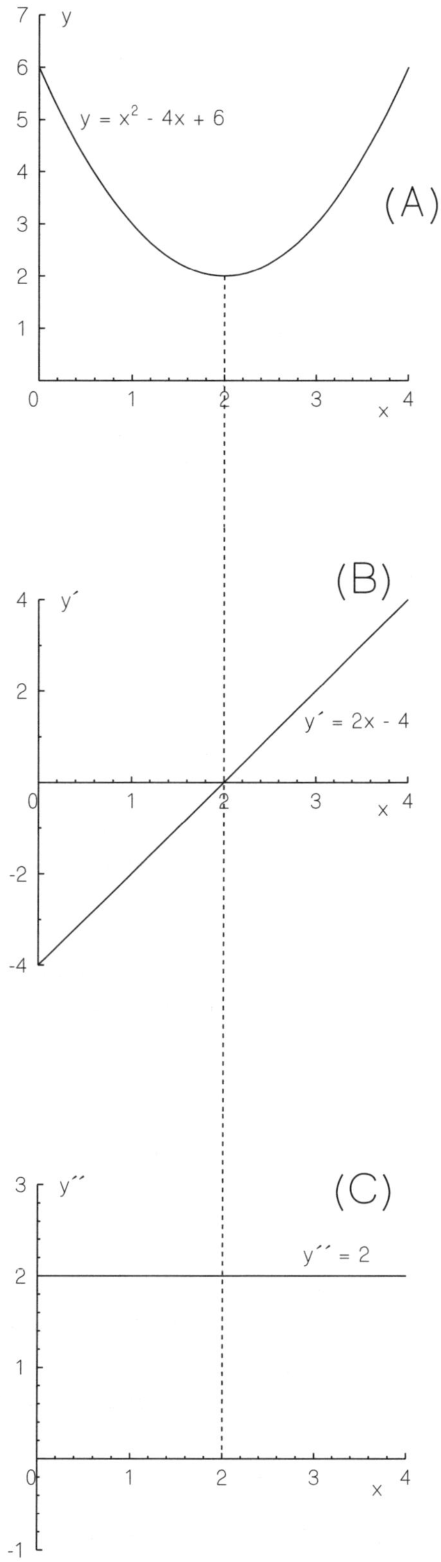

Figure 5-3
Minimization: a geometric interpretation.

The second derivative is positive, which confirms that we have found a minimum value for y, the minimum for average cost.

Figure 5-3 contains the graphs of the original function in panel A, the first derivative in panel B, and the second derivative in panel C. Since the derivative in panel B equals zero at $x = 2$, the original function must be a maximum or a minimum at that x-value. The first derivative in panel B is negative in value for $x < 2$, zero for x = 2, and positive for x > 2. Therefore, the original function must have a negative slope for x-values less than 2 and a positive slope for x-values greater than 2, meaning that the original function must be a minimum at x = 2. Finally, the slope of the first derivative is positive, since the second derivative exceeds zero ($y'' = 2$), which again means that the original function must go from a negative slope to a positive slope as x passes through x = 2, confirming that y = f(x) is a minimum at x = 2.

5-3 Some Refinements and Exceptions

5-3a Relative Maxima and Minima

The procedures described in the first two sections of this chapter apply generally to finding relative maxima and minima; they do not necessarily identify absolute[3] maximum or minimum points.

Definition: A function has a relative (or local) maximum at x = a if:

$$f(a) \geq f(a + r)$$

for "small" positive or negative values of r. This means that the function f(x) is larger at x = a than it is at values of x that are larger or smaller than a, but in the "neighborhood" of a.

Definition: A function has a relative (or local) minimum at x = a if:

$$f(a) \leq f(a + r)$$

for "small" positive or negative values of r. This means that the function f(x) is smaller at x = a than it is at values of x that are larger or smaller than a, but in the neighborhood of a.

The word relative (or local) is used to distinguish between that point and an absolute maximum or minimum. If the point in question is an absolute maximum, the following holds for all x and not just for all x close to a:

$$f(a) \geq f(x)$$

An example should make this clear. Consider the graph in Figure 5-4 of the following equation:

$$y = f(x) = x^3 - 1.5x^2 - 6x + 20 \qquad (5\text{-}6)$$

At x = 2, the function reaches a relative minimum (y = 10), since values of x in the neighborhood of x = 2 would produce larger values for y = f(x). However, for sufficiently large negative values of x, the function decreases without limit. Indeed, this function has no absolute minimum as long as there are no restrictions on the domain of x. At x = –1, the function reaches a relative maximum (y = 23.5), since values in the neighborhood of x = –1 would produce smaller values for y = f(x). But for sufficiently large positive values of x, the function increases without limit. Hence, the function has neither an absolute minimum nor an absolute maximum.

To show that the methods outlined earlier would identify the two relative extreme values shown in Figure 5-4, first differentiate Equation 5-6 and set the result equal to zero:

3. Absolute maximum or minimum points are sometimes called *global* maximum or minimum points.

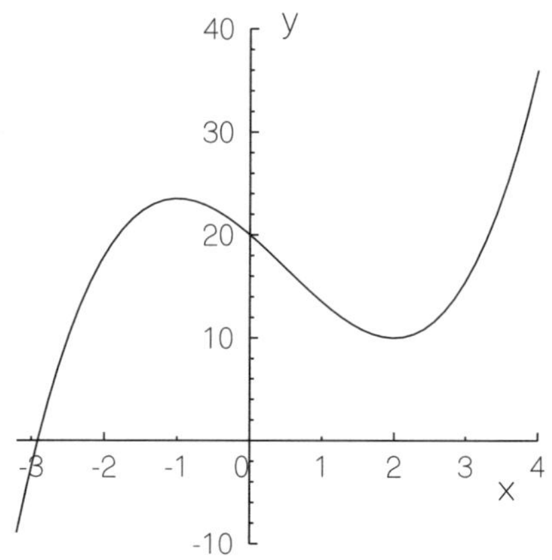

Figure 5-4
Graph of
$y = x^3 - 1.5x^2 - 6x + 20$.

$$\frac{dy}{dx} = 3x^2 - 3x - 6 = 0$$
$$= 3(x^2 - x - 2) = 0$$
$$= 3(x - 2)(x + 1) = 0$$

The solution values (or critical roots) are x = 2 and x = –1. So far, we know that the slope of the primitive function is zero at x = 2 and x = –1. To determine whether these represent maximum or minimum values, compute the second derivative:

$$\frac{d^2y}{dx^2} = 6x - 3$$

and substitute x = 2:

$$\frac{d^2y}{dx^2} = 6(2) - 3 = 9$$

which is positive, so the primitive function is concave upward; therefore, the primitive function is a relative minimum at x = 2. Next, substitute x = –1 into the second derivative:

$$\frac{d^2y}{dx^2} = 6(-1) - 3 = -9$$

which is negative, so the primitive function is concave downward, confirming that the primitive function is a relative maximum at x = –1.

Suppose we restrict the domain of x, so that $0 \le x \le 3$. The relative minimum at x = 2 would be the absolute minimum as well. However, for this domain no relative maximum exists, according to the definition above, but an absolute maximum exists at x = 0, where y = 20. (Confirm that y = 15.5 for x = 3.) Positions such these are known as "end point" extreme values, and they are generally of little relevance in economic analysis. The domain for independent variables of functions we want to maximize usually is restricted; negative values for output or amounts of goods consumed are not sensible, and when constraints are added the practical domain of the function we want to maximize or minimize is often relatively small. For these reasons, in microeconomics we are almost exclusively interested in relative extreme values; therefore, our methods for finding such values are those outlined in sections 5-1 and 5-2 and generalized in the following sections. Finally, recognize that relative extreme values are often absolute extreme values as well without any restriction on the domain of x. The examples presented in sections 5-1 and 5-2 are cases in which the extreme values found by traditional methods are also the absolute extreme values.

5-3b Points of Inflection

A point of inflection, where concavity changes, may possess a first derivative that is equal to zero, but is not a relative maximum or minimum. An example will make this clear. Consider the function shown in Equation 5-7:

$$y = \tfrac{1}{3}x^3 - 2x^2 + 4x \qquad (5\text{-}7)$$

Calculate the first derivative and set it equal to zero in order to find the relative extreme value(s):

$$\frac{dy}{dx} = x^2 - 4x + 4 = 0$$
$$= (x - 2)(x - 2) = 0$$

so the solution value is x = 2. If the second derivative is negative at x = 2, the relative extreme value is a maximum, and if the second derivative is positive for x = 2, the relative extreme value is a minimum. Computing the second derivative yields the following:

$$\frac{d^2y}{dx^2} = 2x - 4$$

and at x = 2, the second derivative is zero. If the second derivative is zero when the first derivative is zero, the second derivative test fails. If we test the first derivative on either side of x = 2, we will find that the slope of the primitive function (Equation 5-7) is positive on both sides. This is clear from the graph of the function in Figure 5-5; as x passes through 2, the slope is positive on both sides, but the concavity of the function changes from concave downward to concave upward.

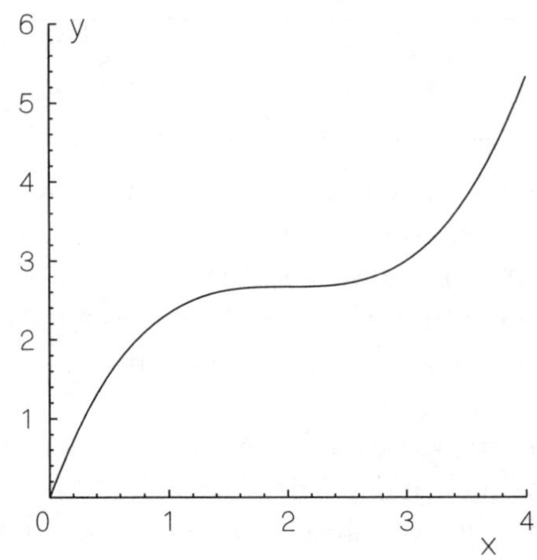

Figure 5-5
Graph of $y = \tfrac{1}{3}x^3 - 2x^2 + 4x$.

To generalize, if the first derivative is zero at x = a and the second derivative is also zero at x = a, the value of the function may be a relative maximum, a relative minimum, or a point of inflection. The first derivative must be tested for the sign of the slope on either side of x = a, to determine which of these conditions apply. The second derivative test is typically more convenient than evaluating the first derivative on each side of the suspected extreme value, and it usually provides an unequivocal conclusion for relative maximum or minimum, the exception being (as just discussed) where the second derivative is zero.

5-3c A Discontinuous First Derivative

Another exception to the general procedures for finding maxima and minima is the possibility of a discontinuous first derivative at a minimum or maximum. Suppose the function under consideration is as shown in Equation 5-8:

$$y = (x-1)^{2/3} + 2 \qquad (5\text{-}8)$$

The first derivative of 5.8 is

$$\frac{dy}{dx} = \frac{2}{3(x-1)^{1/3}}$$

which is discontinuous at x = 1, since division by zero is not allowed. This function has a relative minimum at x = 1, but the first derivative is not equal to zero at the minimum. This function is graphed in Figure 5-6. Clearly, the function does possess a relative minimum at x = 1, but since the first derivative is not zero at this point, the first derivative test fails. In order to find the relative minimum depicted in Figure 5-6, we would examine those points for which the derivative fails to exist for a possible maximum or minimum. This can be accomplished by evaluating the first derivative on either side of the discontinuity.

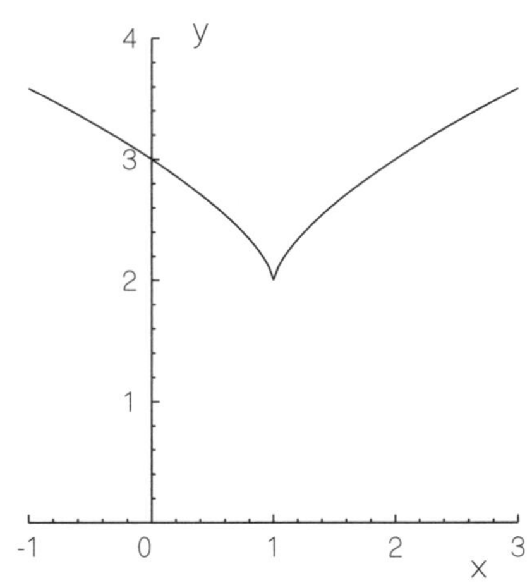

Figure 5-6
Graph of $y = (x - 1)^{2/3} + 2$.

5-4 A Generalization

The refinements and exceptions presented in section 5-3 are just that. The general rules for finding maxima and minima are adequate except in unusual circumstances. In economics it is usually relative extremum for which we are searching, and a failure of the first derivative to detect an extreme value is rare. In addition, the second derivative will usually distinguish between a maximum and a minimum. However, to be (even briefly) complete, such exceptions must be considered. Having done that, we can now generalize the procedures that apply in the vast majority of cases.

In economics, the procedures for finding extreme values, maxima or minima, are typically called *optimization*, since we are searching for values that are "best" in some economic context; the maximum profit, maximum utility, or minimum level of cost all carry best or optimal connotations. The optimization procedures are the identical procedures for finding extreme values outlined above. To generalize, these are the procedures for finding extreme (optimal) values:

First. Given that y = f(x) is the quantity for which we want to find a maximum, find the values of x for which

$$\frac{dy}{dx} = y' = 0$$

Second. Test each value of x for which dy/dx = 0, for a maximum, a minimum, or neither. There are two commonly applied tests:

The first derivative test. If the first derivative changes sign as x passes through the suspected value (say, x = a) at which y = f(x) may be an extreme value, then a relative extreme value indeed exists. Specifically, if

$$\frac{dy}{dx} \text{ is positive for } x < a$$

and

$$\frac{dy}{dx} \text{ is negative for } x > a$$

then a relative maximum exists for y = f(x) at x = a.

And if

$$\frac{dy}{dx} \text{ is negative for } x < a$$

and

$$\frac{dy}{dx} \text{ is positive for } x > a$$

then a relative minimum exists for y = f(x) at x = a.

The second derivative test. If the second derivative is negative when the first derivative is zero, a relative maximum exists, and if the second derivative is positive when the first derivative is zero, a relative minimum exists. Symbolically, if

$$\frac{d^2y}{dx^2} \text{ is negative when}$$

$$\frac{dy}{dx} = 0,$$

y is a relative maximum.

And if

$$\frac{d^2y}{dx^2} \text{ is positive when}$$

$$\frac{dy}{dx} = 0,$$

y is a relative minimum.

If the second derivative is zero when the first derivative is zero, the second derivative test fails.

Third. If the derivative does not exist (is not defined) at some point, examine that point as a possible maximum or minimum (refer to Figure 5-6).

Fourth. Recognize that the maximum and minimum values found by the preceding methods are not necessarily absolute (global) maximum and minimum values. If the function is defined for a limited domain for x, examine the end points of that domain for extreme values.

As a final note for this section, it is often obvious from the function itself or from economic theory that the function for which we want to find an extreme value is everywhere differentiable and the extreme value we want to find is not at an end point. In these cases, the extreme value will be an interior point where the first derivative is zero. Therefore, if we find the one point where the derivative is zero, we will have the extreme value (maximum or minimum) we are searching for and there will be no need for a second-derivative test or the equivalent. The examples of the profit function in section 5-1 and the average cost function in section 5-2 meet these criteria.

5-5 A Necessary Digression for Sufficient Understanding of Extrema

The procedures outlined in the preceding sections of this chapter bring into focus the concepts of necessary versus sufficient conditions. These terms are often used in mathematics and economics to describe a situation where a first condition, a necessary condition, *must* be present in order for some relationship to hold, but the presence of the first condition does not *ensure* that the relationship holds. A second condition, the sufficient condition, *guarantees* that the relationship holds. From the previous discussion of maximum and minimum points, the necessary condition for, say, a maximum is that the first derivative must equal zero. However, this point may not be a maximum. It could be a point of inflection or it could be a minimum. If the second derivative is negative when the first derivative is zero, this is sufficient evidence for the maximum. Alternatively, when the first derivative is zero, the sign of the derivative changing from positive to negative as x passes through the value at which the derivative is zero serves as sufficient evidence of a maximum.

At the risk of introducing too much terminology, in economics, the condition that the first derivative must be zero for the value of x at which we suspect $y = f(x)$ to be an extreme value is usually called the *first-order condition.* The second derivative test is known as the *second-order condition.* These relationships are summarized in Table 5-1.

TABLE 5-1 First-Order and Second-Order Conditions for Extrema

Condition	Maximum	Minimum
first order (necessary)	$\frac{dy}{dx} = 0$	$\frac{dy}{dx} = 0$
second order (sufficient)	$\frac{d^2y}{dx^2} < 0$	$\frac{d^2y}{dx^2} < 0$

5-6 Maxima and Minima: Functions of Two Independent Variables

The previous sections showed how to use calculus to solve maximum and minimum problems for functions of a single variable. Many of the concepts in microeconomics require functions of two or more independent variables. This section presents methods for finding extreme values for functions of more than one independent variable.

Suppose we want to find the extreme values for a surface represented by Equation 5-9:

$$z = f(x,y) \tag{5-9}$$

Suppose further that the function is continuous and has continuous partial derivatives for some region in the xy plane. The function z = f(x,y) will have a relative maximum at point (a,b) if Equation 5-10 holds for "small" positive or negative values of r and t.

$$f(a, b) \geq f(a + r, b + t) \tag{5-10}$$

This means that the function f(x,y) is larger at x = a, y = b than it is for values of x and y smaller than a and larger than b, but in the neighborhood of (a,b). If the inequality in Equation 5-10 holds for all points in the region, the function has an absolute or global maximum at the point (a,b). If the inequality (≥) is reversed (≤), the function would have a minimum value, either relative or absolute at the point (a,b).

Consider the surface in Figure 5-7, which is given by Equation 5-11:

$$z = 10x - x^2 + 10y - y^2 \tag{5-11}$$

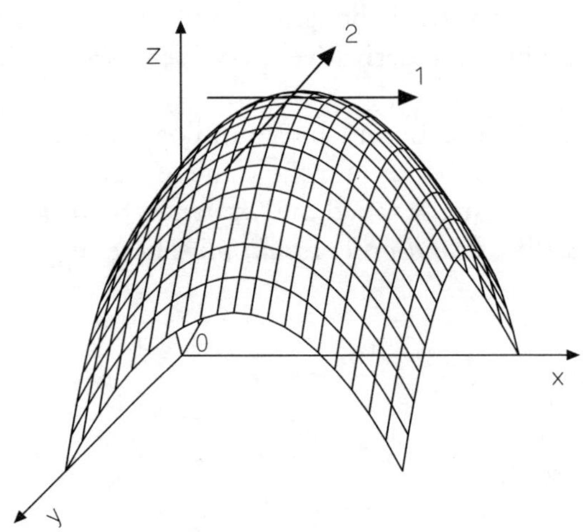

Figure 5-7
Graph of
$z = 10x - x^2 + 10y - y^2$.

In the graph, the maximum occurs at an interior point over the region. Notice that there is but one point where the function is a maximum, and that point is where the two arrows (1) and (2) intersect. Arrow (1) is parallel to the xz plane and therefore has a slope of zero with respect to the x axis as viewed from the z axis. Many other arrows could also have zero slope relative to the xz plane and be tangent to the surface (if the arrow is kept parallel to the x axis and tangent to the surface but pulled forward or pushed backward along the y axis), but only one is at the maximum value for the function. Arrow (2) is parallel to the yz plane and tangent to the surface (meaning that it has a slope of zero with respect to the y axis when viewed from the z axis). When arrow (2) intersects arrow (1), that point is the maximum for the function z. Thus, the criteria for the maximum for this function are that arrows (1) and (2) on the surface of the function must have slopes of zero with respect to the xz and yz planes, respectively, and they must intersect each other.

5-6a First-Order Condition

In terms of calculus, the condition stated in Equation 5-12 must hold for an extreme value to exist.

$$\frac{\partial z}{\partial x} = \frac{\partial z}{\partial y} = 0 \qquad (5\text{-}12)$$

Equation 5-12 is the first-order condition for a maximum of a function of two independent variables. It is a necessary but not a sufficient condition for an extreme value. This first-order condition fails to distinguish between extreme values and *saddle points* or points of inflection. Since we have considered points of inflection in reference to functions of a single independent variable, here we consider the problems involved when the surface has a saddle point. Such a surface is depicted in Figure 5-8 and is given by Equation 5-13:

$$z = x^2 - y^2 \qquad (5\text{-}13)$$

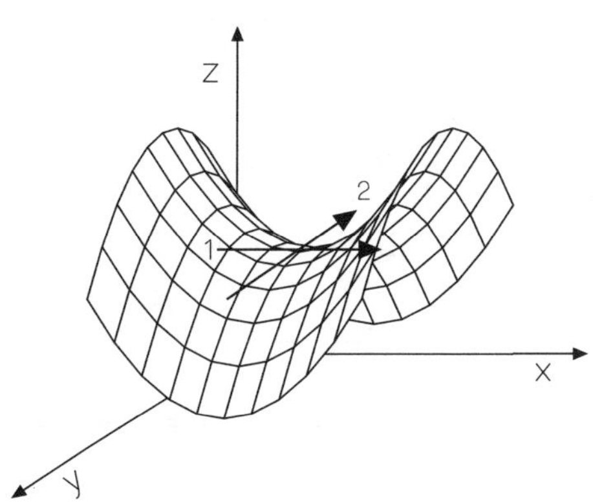

Figure 5-8
Graph of $z = x^2 - y^2$.

Here the arrows (1) and (2) are again tangent to the surface and they intersect. The point of intersection, however, is not a maximum, nor is it a minimum. It is known as a *saddle point*, for obvious reasons. The problem encountered here is that the saddle point is a minimum with respect to one variable and a maximum with respect to the other variable. If we travel in the direction of arrow (2), up the surface from the bottom to the intersection with arrow (1) and then down the other side, we seem to have reached a maximum. On the other hand, if we travel in the direction of arrow (1), down the surface from the top left to the intersection of the arrows and then back up again, we seem to have reached a minimum.

Clearly, criteria other than first-order conditions are necessary to establish maxima and minima for functions of two variables.

5-6b Second-Order Condition

The second-order condition for a maximum of a function of two independent variables involves second derivatives of the primitive function. The following notation will aid in our discussion. If we have a function, $z = f(x,y)$, the first derivative with respect to x is expressed symbolically as

$$\frac{\partial z}{\partial x} = f_x$$

and the second derivative with respect to x is defined as

$$\frac{\partial^2 z}{\partial x^2} = f_{xx}$$

Similarly, the first and second derivatives of z with respect to y are designated by these symbolic expressions:

$$\frac{\partial z}{\partial y} = f_y$$

$$\frac{\partial^2 z}{\partial y^2} = f_{yy}$$

It is also possible to differentiate the function $z = f(x,y)$ with respect to one variable and then differentiate the result with respect to the other. These are known as *cross partial derivatives* and are designated f_{yx} and f_{xy}. The expression f_{yx} means that the function was partially differentiated with respect to y, and that result was partially differentiated with respect to x, and f_{xy} means that the order was reversed. For most of the functions that will be encountered at this level, $f_{yx} = f_{xy}$. *Young's Theorem*[4] states that if the two cross partial derivatives are continuous, they will also be identical; that is, the order of differentiation is immaterial.

Using the notation from above, the second-order conditions for extreme values can be stated. Assuming that the first-order conditions have been met ($f_x = f_y = 0$), the following will be sufficient for finding a maximum or a minimum:

Maximum

(a) $f_{xx} < 0$ *and* $f_{yy} < 0$

and

(b) $(f_{xx})(f_{yy}) - (f_{xy})^2 > 0$

For a maximum, the second partials must be less than zero (which is consistent with the second derivative test for functions of one independent variable), but the product of the second partials minus the square of the cross partials must be greater than zero.

4. For a proof of Young's Theorem, see George B. Thomas, *Calculus and Analytical Geometry* (Reading, MA: Addison-Wesley, 1966, pp. 705–707).

Minimum

(a) $f_{xx} > 0$ and $f_{yy} > 0$

and

(b) $(f_{xx})(f_{yy}) - (f_{xy})^2 > 0$

For a minimum, the second partials must be greater than zero (as we would expect) and the product of the second partials minus the square of the cross partials again must be greater than zero.

If part (b) of the second-order condition is less than zero, a saddle point has been located. Finally, if part (b) is equal to zero, the test fails. In this case, points in the neighborhood of the suspected extreme value should be examined to determine whether the point in question is an extreme value.

Example 1

Applying these techniques to find the maximum depicted earlier in Figure 5-7, we proceed as follows. Restating Equation 5-11:

$$z = 10x - x^2 + 10y - y^2$$

Find the partial derivatives with respect to x and y and set each equal to zero for the *first-order condition*:

$$\frac{\partial z}{\partial x} = f_x = 10 - 2x = 0$$

$$\frac{\partial z}{\partial y} = f_y = 10 - 2y = 0$$

The solution values are then x = 5 and y = 5, meaning that the point (5,5) may be a maximum or a minimum. Find the second derivatives and the cross derivatives to apply the *second-order condition*:

$$\frac{\partial^2 z}{\partial x^2} = f_{xx} = -2$$

$$\frac{\partial^2 z}{\partial y^2} = f_{yy} = -2$$

$$f_{xy} = f_{yx} = 0$$

The second derivatives, f_{xx} and f_{yy}, are less than zero, which implies a maximum, but we must still test to see if $(f_{xx})(f_{yy}) - (f_{xy})^2 > 0$:

$$(-2)(-2) - (0)^2 = 4 > 0$$

Since the first-order and second-order conditions are satisfied for a maximum, we can be sure that the point x = 5, y = 5 is a maximum for z. The maximum value for z from Equation 5-11 is as follows:

$$z_{max} = 10(5) - 5^2 + 10(5) - 5^2 = 50$$

Example 2

Suppose we were to test Equation 5-13, repeated for convenience below, for extreme values.

$$z = x^2 - y^2$$

Find the partial derivatives with respect to x and y and set each equal to zero for the *first-order condition*:

$$\frac{\partial z}{\partial x} = f_x = 2x = 0$$

$$\frac{\partial z}{\partial y} = f_y = -2y = 0$$

The solution values are $x = 0$ and $y = 0$, meaning that the point (0,0) may be a maximum or a minimum. Next, find the second derivatives and the cross derivative to apply the *second-order condition*:

$$\frac{\partial^2 z}{\partial x^2} = f_{xx} = 2$$

$$\frac{\partial^2 z}{\partial y^2} = f_{yy} = -2$$

$$f_{xy} = f_{yx} = 0$$

The second derivatives, f_{xx} and f_{yy} are differently signed, and $(f_{xx})(f_{yy}) - (f_{xy})^2 < 0$:

$$(2)(-2) - (0)^2 = -4 < 0$$

Therefore, the point (0,0) is a saddle point. (This is the saddle point shown in Figure 5-8. The careful reader will notice that the saddle point in the graph does not seem to be where $x = 0$ and $y = 0$. This is because the z-axis intersects both the x and y axes at negative values, so the saddle point indeed occurs at $x = 0$, $y = 0$.)

Example 3

Examine Equation 5-14 for extreme values. The two partial derivatives, f_x and f_y, must hold simultaneously. From f_y, $x = 2y$; substituting 2y in place of x in f_x, yields $y = 3$. And if $y = 3$, $x = 6$, from either Equation 5-15 or 5-16.

$$z = x^2 - xy + y^2 - 9x + 50 \qquad (5\text{-}14)$$

$$\frac{\partial z}{\partial x} = f_x = 2x - y - 9 = 0 \qquad (5\text{-}15)$$

$$\frac{\partial z}{\partial y} = f_y = -x + 2y = 0 \qquad (5\text{-}16)$$

Next, find the second derivatives and the cross derivative(s) to apply the second-order condition:

$$\frac{\partial^2 z}{\partial x^2} = f_{xx} = 2$$

$$\frac{\partial^2 z}{\partial y^2} = f_{yy} = 2 \text{ and}$$

$$f_{xy} = f_{yx} = -1$$

The second derivatives, f_{xx} and f_{yy}, are both positive, which implies a minimum, and, since $(f_{xx})(f_{yy}) - (f_{xy})^2 > 0$:

$$(2)(2) - (-1)^2 = 3 > 0$$

the point (6,3) is established as a minimum.

5-7 Maxima and Minima Subject to Constraints

As stated in the introduction to this chapter, many important microeconomic problems involve maximization or minimization of some objective function subject to a constraint. The most common of these problems include utility maximization subject to a budget constraint (budget line), output maximization subject to a cost constraint (iso-cost line), and cost minimization subject to a production constraint.

5-7a A Method of Substitution

Suppose we are given a utility function U = xy, where U = total utility, x = quantity of good x consumed, and y = quantity of good y consumed. Suppose further that the price of x is \$1 per unit ($p_x = 1$) the price of y is \$2 per unit ($p_y = 2$), and the consumer has \$100 of income (I = 100) to spend on the two goods. The general formula for the budget constraint is $I = p_x x + p_y y$. We want to maximize Equation 5-17 subject to the constraint in Equation 5-18:

$$U = xy \qquad (5\text{-}17)$$

$$100 = 1x + 2y \qquad (5\text{-}18)$$

One approach to this problem is to solve Equation 5-18 for x (or y) and substitute the result into Equation 5-17. Here x = 100 – 2y, and therefore Equation 5-18 becomes

$$U = (100 - 2y)y = 100y - 2y^2 \qquad (5\text{-}17')$$

Now differentiate Equation 5-17′ with respect to y and set the result equal to zero:

$$dU/dy = 100 - 4y = 0$$

Solving for y:

$$y = 25$$

If y = 25, from Equation 5-18, x = 50. Finally, we know that y = 25 and x = 50 is a (constrained) maximum for U, since $d^2U/dy^2 = -4$.

This method of substitution works quite well when there is only one constraint and the constraint is uncomplicated (easily solved for one of the variables in terms of the other). A more flexible method with important analytical advantages is more frequently used for constrained extremum. That method is known as the *Lagrange-multiplier method.*

5-7b The Lagrange-Multiplier Method

Under the Lagrange-multiplier approach, the constraint is incorporated into the objective function so that the procedures for unconstrained maxima and minima can be applied. Using the example from the previous section, where U = xy is to be maximized subject to 100 = 1x + 2y (which may also be written as x + 2y – 100 = 0 or 100 – x – 2y = 0), we write the Lagrangian function as shown in Equation 5-19:

$$L = xy - \lambda(x + 2y - 100) \qquad (5\text{-}19)$$

where λ is known as the *Lagrange undetermined multiplier.*[5] In Equation 5-19, λ is treated as an additional variable, so when we take the first derivatives and set them equal to zero, we differentiate L with respect to x, y, and λ.

Proceeding, the expressions in Equations 5-20, 5-21, and 5-22 are obtained:

$$L_x = y - \lambda = 0 \qquad (5\text{-}20)$$

$$L_y = x - 2\lambda = 0 \qquad (5\text{-}21)$$

$$L_\lambda = 100 - x - 2y = 0 \qquad (5\text{-}22)$$

Two important points should be emphasized here. First, these three simultaneous equations represent the first-order condition for an extreme value. Second, Equation 5-22 simply restates the budget constraint, requiring that the restraint be satisfied.

Solving the three first derivative equations simultaneously, we obtain x = 50, y = 25, and λ = 25. These values are found as follows.

From Equation 5-20:

$$\lambda = y$$

From Equation 5-21:

$$\lambda = x/2$$

Therefore, since $\lambda = \lambda$,

$$y = x/2$$

or

$$x = 2y$$

5. In our expression, the *Lagrange-multiplier* is written with a minus (–) sign in front. The results will be the same if the expression is written with a plus (+) sign. Since the constraint will equal zero, it does not matter whether we add or subtract zero.

Substitute 2y for x in Equation 5-22 and solve for y = 25. Then x = 50 in Equation 5-22 if y = 25. Finally, substitute y = 25 into Equation 5-20, to obtain $\lambda = 25$.

Generalizing the above procedure is straightforward. Given an objective function, as shown in Equation 5-23:

$$z = f(x,y) \qquad (5\text{-}23)$$

subject to the constraint shown in Equation 5-24

$$g(x,y) = k \qquad (5\text{-}24)$$

where k is some constant, the Lagrangian function is written as follows:

$$L = f(x,y) - \lambda[k - g(x,y)]$$

First-Order Condition

The first-order condition is shown in Equations 5-25, 5-26, and 5-27, where the subscripts attached to L, f, and g indicate the partial derivative of those functions with respect to the subscript:

$$L_x = f_x + \lambda g_x = 0 \qquad (5\text{-}25)$$

$$L_y = f_y + \lambda g_y = 0 \qquad (5\text{-}26)$$

$$L_\lambda = k - g(x,y) = 0 \qquad (5\text{-}27)$$

When the three expressions above are solved simultaneously for x, y, and λ, an extreme value for the objective function *may* have been found. The statement above emphasizes that an extreme value *may* have been found, because we have yet to state the second-order conditions.

Second-Order Conditions[6]

The second-order conditions for constrained maximum and minimum values are similar to the unconstrained case, but with several important differences, as we now explain. Assuming that the first-order conditions have been met ($L_x = L_y = L_\lambda = 0$), the following will be sufficient for finding a maximum or a minimum:

Maximum

(a) $L_{xx} < 0$ and $L_{yy} < 0$

(b) $(L_{xx})(L_{yy}) - (L_{xy})^2 > 0$

For a maximum to be assured, (a) the second partials must be less than zero (which is consistent with the second derivative test for functions of one independent variable), but in addition, (b) the product of the partials minus the square of the cross partials must be greater than zero.

6. The second-order conditions are stated here without the aid of matrix algebra. For a treatment of second-order conditions in matrix form, see Alpha C. Chiang, *Fundamental Methods of Mathematical Economics* (New York: McGraw-Hill, 1984, pp. 379–385).

Minimum

$$(a)\ L_{xx} > 0 \text{ and } L_{yy} > 0$$

$$(b)\ (L_{xx})(L_{yy}) - (L_{xy})^2 > 0$$

For a minimum to be assured, the second partials must be greater than zero (as we would expect) and the product of the partials minus the square of the cross partials again must be greater than zero.

If part (b) of the second-order condition is less than or equal to zero, the test fails. Points in the neighborhood of the suspected extreme value should be examined to determine whether the point in question is, in fact, an extreme value. In the case of unconstrained extremum, if part (b) were less than zero, a saddle point would be indicated; that is not the case with constrained extremum. In fact, an extreme point may exist if part (b) is equal to or less than zero. When this occurs, values for x and y in the neighborhood of the suspected extreme point must be examined to determine whether an extreme point does exist. Two additional examples will make some of these points more clear.

Example 1

Examine Equation 5-28 for maxima or minima:

$$z = x^2 + 4y^2 - xy \tag{5-28}$$

subject to the constraint shown in Equation 5-29:

$$x + 2y = 100 \tag{5-29}$$

Form the Lagrangian expression:

$$L = x^2 + 4y^2 - xy - \lambda(100 - x - 2y)$$

Compute the first partial derivatives and set each equal to zero for the *first-order condition*:

$$L_x = 2x - y + \lambda = 0$$

$$L_y = 8y - x + 2\lambda = 0$$

$$L_\lambda = x + 2y - 100 = 0$$

Solve the three equations simultaneously for x, y, and λ:

$$\lambda = y - 2x$$

$$\lambda = \tfrac{1}{2}x - 4y$$

so

$$\tfrac{1}{2}x - 4y = y - 2x$$

and

$$x = 2y$$

Substituting x = 2y into L_λ, solve for y to obtain y = 25. Since x = 2y, x = 50. So the point x = 50, y = 25, is a potential extreme value.

Now compute L_{xx}, L_{yy}, and L_{xy} (= L_{yx}), for the *second-order condition*:

$$L_{xx} = 2$$
$$L_{yy} = 8$$
$$L_{xy} = -1$$

Since the second partial derivatives, L_{xx} and L_{yy}, are positive, a minimum is implied. And since $(2)(8) - (-1)^2 = 15$,

$$(L_{xx})(L_{yy}) - (L_{xy})^2 > 0$$

This means that all the conditions are met for a minimum, so a minimum for the objective function is assured at x = 50, y = 25. The value of z at this point is as follows:

$$z = x^2 + 4y^2 - xy$$
$$z = (50)^2 + 4(25)^2 - (50)(25) = 3,750$$

Example 2

Suppose that a production function for gourmet potato chips is given by the following equation:

$$Q = 10x^{.5}y^{.5}$$

where Q is production in pounds of chips per week, x is potato input (in truckloads), and y is labor input (in persons per week). Now suppose that the firm wants to produce 80 pounds of chips per week and the input cost function is given by the following equation:

$$C = 4x + y$$

where C is costs in hundreds of dollars, the price of raw potatoes is 400 per truckload, and labor is priced at \$100 per week. The objective is to minimize costs, given that the firm wants to produce 80 pounds of chips per week. That is, minimize:

$$C = 4x + y$$

subject to

$$80 = 10x^{.5}y^{.5}$$

Form the Lagrangian expression:

$$L = 4x + y - \lambda(80 - 10x^{.5}y^{.5})$$

Compute the first partial derivatives and set each equal to zero for the *first-order condition*:

$$L_x = 4 + \lambda 5x^{-.5}y^{5} = 0$$

$$L_y = 1 + \lambda 5x^{.5}y^{-.5} = 0$$

$$L_\lambda = -80 + 10x^{.5}y^{.5} = 0$$

Solve the three equations simultaneously for x, y, and λ:

$$\lambda = -.8x^{.5}y^{-.5}$$

$$\lambda = -.2x^{-.5}y^{.5}$$

since

$$\lambda = \lambda$$

$$y = 4x$$

Substitute y = 4x into L_λ and solve for y to obtain y = 16, and since y = 4x, x = 4. So the point x = 4, y = 16 is a potential extreme value. Also, the value of λ can be computed from either expression above; $\lambda = -.4$.

Now compute L_{xx}, L_{yy}, and L_{xy} (= L_{yx}), for the *second-order condition*:

$$L_{xx} = -2.5\lambda x^{-1.5}y^{.5}$$

$$L_{yy} = -2.5\lambda x^{.5}y^{-1.5}$$

$$L_{xy} = \lambda 2.5x^{-.5}y^{-.5}$$

Since the second partial derivatives, L_{xx} and L_{yy} are positive ($\lambda = -.4$), a minimum is implied. Verify, however that:

$$(L_{xx})(L_{yy}) - (L_{xy})^2 = 0$$

This result means that a minimum is not guaranteed for costs when x = 4 and y = 16. The level of costs is 32 ($3,200), since C = 4(4) + 1(16) = 32, but we do not know whether costs have been minimized for an output of 80 pounds of chips per week. The procedure to be followed in a case such as this is to examine points in the neighborhood of the suspected extreme value to see whether we have located a minimum. Often in microeconomics we can also appeal to graphic analysis. Suppose we plot the isoquant for an output of 80 pounds of potatoes per week. That equation, solved for y, would be

$$y = 64/x$$

The accompanying budget line or iso-cost line is as follows when solved for y:

$$y = 32 - 4x$$

Since the isoquant for an output of 80 is tangent to the iso-cost line in Figure 5-9, we know that this output cannot be produced at a lower cost; hence, the minimum for costs has been located.

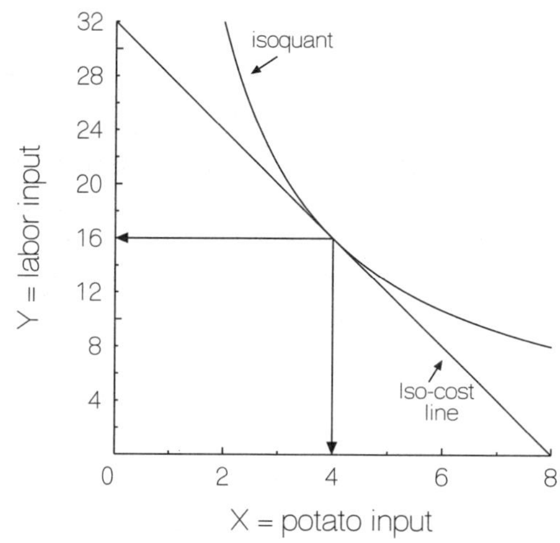

Figure 5-9
Cost minimization.

Some Extensions

The Lagrange-multiplier method can be extended to three (or more) variables. The logical extension for three variables is

$$U = f(x,y,z)$$

with the constraint

$$g(x,y,z) = k$$

Form the Lagrangian expression:

$$L = f(x,y,z) - \lambda[k - g(x,y,z)]$$

The first-order condition for an extreme value is

$$L_x = f_x + \lambda g_x = 0$$
$$L_y = f_y + \lambda g_y = 0$$
$$L_z = f_z + \lambda g_z = 0$$
$$L_\lambda = k - g(x,y,z) = 0$$

These equations would have to be solved simultaneously for x, y, z, and λ to find the point for which the objective function is a maximum or minimum.[7]

7. The second-order conditions are more complicated for these extended cases and are usually stated with the aid of matrix algebra. Here we state only the first-order conditions

Suppose there is an objective function:

$$z = f(x,y)$$

subject to these two constraints:

$$g(x,y) = k$$
$$h(x,y) = m$$

where m, like k, is a constant. Form the Lagrangian expression:

$$L = f(x,y) - \lambda[k - g(x,y)] - \mu[m - h(x,y)]$$

The first-order condition is

$$L_x = f_x + \lambda g_x + \mu h_x = 0$$
$$L_y = f_y + \lambda g_y + \mu h_y = 0$$
$$L_\lambda = k - g(x,y) = 0$$
$$L_\mu = m - h(x,y) = 0$$

In similar fashion, the Lagrange-multiplier technique can be extended to other general cases of more variables and more constraints.

5-8 Summary

This chapter has presented techniques for finding maxima and minima under varied conditions. Extremum of functions of a single variable was extended to functions of more than one variable, and the objective function was also made subject to constraints, the "utility" of which should be obvious for microeconomic analysis.

The type of analysis presented here is often called "classical" optimization, and it is the mainstay of mathematical microeconomic analysis. These methods are not without limitation, however. For example, local versus absolute extrema are not typically distinguished by this methodology. Additionally, and perhaps the most obvious shortcoming of the methods presented here, is the inability to deal with inequality constraints, an area of investigation that is subject to analysis by linear and nonlinear programming. These "classical" techniques are highly revered by economists, however, and have a number of useful analytical advantages in microeconomic application. Chapter 6 applies these techniques to some of the traditional areas of microeconomic analysis.

Problems

1. Find d^2y/dx^2 for each of the following:

   (a) $y = 6x - 3$
   (b) $y' = 4x^2 + 2x - 3$
   (c) $y = (6x^2 + 3)(2x - 1)$
   (d) $y = (2x^2 + 5x)/(2x)$

2. Determine the maximization for each of the following profit functions, where y is profit and x is output. Show proof of the maximization by using the second derivative test. Calculate the levels of profit.

   (a) $y = -2x^2 + 26x - 60$
   (b) $y = -x^3 + 15x^2 - 10$

3. Consider the functions in Problem 2 again. Do either of these functions have a relative minimum? Are the results meaningful in economic terms?

4. The long-run average cost of producing basketballs is given by

$$y = 6x^2 - 24x + 50$$

where y is costs per ball in dollars and x is number of balls produced per year. Determine where costs are a minimum.

5. Find relative maxima and minima for these equations.

(a) $y = x^3 + x^2 - x - 6$
(b) $y = \frac{2}{3}x^3 - 2x^2 - 30x + 60$

6. Find the maxima and minima, if any, for the following functions. Use second-order conditions to discriminate between maxima and minima.

(a) $z = y^2 + xy + x^2 + 3y - 3x + 10$
(b) $z = 60x - 2x^2 + 100y - y^2$
(c) $z = x^2 - 2y^2 + 12y$
(d) $z = x^2 + y^2 - 2y + 1$

7. Use the Lagrangian method to find the extreme values of the following functions subject to their side conditions (constraints).

(a) $z = x^2 - y^2 + xy$, subject to $2x - y = 0$
(b) $u = 3xy$, subject to $2x + 3y = 100$

Chapter 6

Microeconomic Applications of Extremum

This chapter presents some useful microeconomic applications of the techniques presented in Chapter 5, "Maximization and Minimization." Along the way, some of the concepts of microeconomics should become more clear.

Outline

6-1 A Revenue Maximization Problem

Suppose you have just written the next great American novel. Your publisher has agreed to pay you 20% of the value of *total sales.* The greater the value of total expenditure on the book, the greater your royalties. In other words, it is to your advantage that the price of the book be set so as to maximize total revenue to the publisher. Because of your training in microeconomics, you are asked for pricing advice on your book. The publisher, experienced in marketing this type of book, expects the monthly demand curve to be given by Equation 6-1:

$$P = 100/Q + 50 - Q \qquad (6\text{-}1)$$

Since total revenue is given by Equation 6-2, because total revenue equals price times quantity (TR = PQ).

$$TR = 100 + 50Q - Q^2 \qquad (6\text{-}2)$$

In order to maximize your royalties, you would choose the price and quantity that will maximize Equation 6-2. The procedure is straightforward. Differentiate Equation 6-2 with respect to Q, and set the result (marginal revenue) equal to zero. Solve for Q, substituting that result into Equation 6-1 to find P. Differentiating yields Equation 6-3.

$$d(TR)/dQ = MR = 50 - 2Q = 0 \qquad (6\text{-}3)$$

$$Q = 25$$

From Equation 6-1,

$$P = 100/25 + 50 - 25 = 29$$

Since the second derivative is negative,

$$d^2(TR)/dQ^2 = -2$$

the point in which P = 29 and Q = 25 is a maximum for TR. The level of revenues each month is PQ = 725, of which you receive 20% or $145. (Don't quit your day job yet!)

As a student of microeconomics, you know by now that revenue is maximized where the price elasticity of demand is equal to one, for demand curves that have such a point. We will now verify that the point chosen for revenue maximization is where $\eta_d = 1$. The formula for price elasticity is given by Equation 6-4:

$$\eta_d = -\frac{dQ}{dP} \cdot \frac{P}{Q} \qquad (6\text{-}4)$$

The formula calls for dQ/dP, and our demand curve is written with P as the dependent variable. Simply differentiate Equation 6-1 with respect to Q to obtain:

$$dP/dQ = -100/Q^2 - 1 = (-100 - Q^2)/Q^2$$

therefore,

$$dQ/dP = -Q^2/(100 + Q^2)$$

Remember from Chapter 4, "Microeconomic Applications of Derivatives," that this inverse function procedure applies for monotonic functions and this demand curve is monotonically decreasing. Substituting into Equation 6-4,

$$\eta_d = -\frac{-(25^2)}{100 + 25^2} \cdot \frac{29}{25} = 1$$

Your recommendation to the publisher that the price of the book be set at \$29 per copy to maximize revenues (and royalties) is in accord with what we know about price elasticity of demand.

6-2 Profit Maximization

Your publisher is interested in maximizing profit, not revenue. Suppose the costs of publishing and marketing the book are given by the simple cost equation shown in Equation 6-5:

$$TC = 100 + 10Q \tag{6-5}$$

Profit (π) equals TR – TC or

$$\pi = 100 + 50Q - Q^2 - 100 - 10Q \tag{6-6}$$

To maximize profit, differentiate Equation 6-6 with respect to Q, set the result equal to zero, and solve for Q and then P as shown in Equation 6-7:

$$d\pi/dQ = 50 - 2Q - 10 = 0 \tag{6-7}$$

$$Q = 20$$

From Equation 6-1,

$$P = 100/20 + 50 - 20 = 35$$

The second derivative is the same as the preceding:

$$d^2(TR)/dQ^2 = -2$$

which is negative, so the point at which P = 35 and Q = 20 is a maximum, this time for profit (π). The level of profit for the publisher is

$$\pi = 100 + 50(20) - 20^2 - 100 - 10(20) = 400$$

Total revenue, PQ, is \$700, and your royalties in this case are \$140 per month. Also, verify that the publisher's profit would have been \$375, in section 6-1, where the objective is to maximize sales. There are two points to be gleaned from this section and the previous one:

- Maximizing total revenue and maximizing profit are not the same, except where marginal cost is zero.
- The author's and the publisher's incentives are in conflict where pricing policy is concerned if royalties are based on the total value of sales (although it is to their mutual benefit that the book do well in general).

6-3 Lagrangian Utility Maximization

In this section, the conditions for utility maximization using the Lagrange-multiplier technique are repeated for the general case with some economic interpretations. The specific case of a Cobb-Douglas utility function is presented and the demand and income consumption curves are derived.

6-3a A Generalization with Economic Interpretations

The Lagrange-multiplier technique, which was introduced in Chapter 5, "Maximization and Minimization," has a number of useful interpretations when applied to utility maximization. Suppose utility is a function of two goods, economics classes (C) and skiing trips (S):

$$U = U(C, S)$$

The budget constraint is given by Equation 6-8:

$$I = P_C C + P_S S \tag{6-8}$$

The Lagrangian expression is shown in Equation 6-9:

$$L = U(C, S) - \lambda(P_C C + P_S S - I) \tag{6-9}$$

First-order conditions require partially differentiating Equation 6-8 with respect to C, S, and λ, and setting each derivative equal to zero (see Equations 6-10, 6-11, and 6-12 below):

$$\partial L/\partial C = \partial U/\partial C - \lambda P_C = 0 \tag{6-10}$$

$$\partial L/\partial S = \partial U/\partial S - \lambda P_S = 0 \tag{6-11}$$

$$\partial L/\partial \lambda = I - P_C C - P_S S = 0 \tag{6-12}$$

Dividing Equation 6-10 by Equation 6-11 yields Equation 6-13:

$$\frac{\partial U/\partial C}{\partial U/\partial S} = \frac{P_C}{P_S} \tag{6-13}$$

The left-hand side of Equation 6-13 is the ratio of the marginal utilities of economics classes to skiing trips, which is also the marginal rate of substitution (of C for S), and minus the slope of a given indifference curve. The right-hand side of 6-13 is the price ratio (P_C/P_S), which is equal to minus the slope of the budget line. For consumer equilibrium, the marginal rate of substitution of C for S must equal the price ratio, P_C/P_S.

Figure 6-1 shows these relationships graphically. The slope of an indifference curve at any given point is (minus) the marginal rate of substitution of the variable on the x axis for the variable on the y axis. The slope of the budget line is (minus) the ratio of the price of a good on the x axis to the price of the good on the y axis. For equilibrium, the slopes must be the same. This occurs in the diagram only at a point of *tangency*, the point E in the diagram.

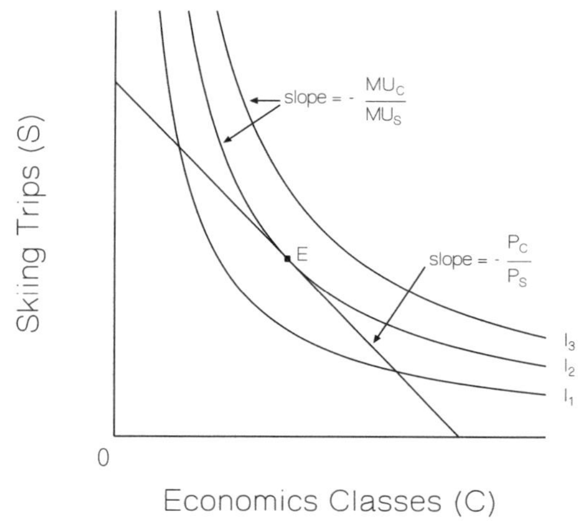

Figure 6-1
Consumer equilibrium.

If Equations 6-10 and 6-11 are solved for λ, we would have the following expression:

$$\lambda = \frac{\partial U/\partial C}{P_C} = \frac{\partial U/\partial S}{P_S}$$

or

$$\lambda = \frac{MU_C}{P_C} = \frac{MU_S}{P_S}$$

where $\partial U/\partial C = MU_C$ is the marginal utility of economics classes and $\partial U/\partial S = MU_S$ is the marginal utility of skiing trips. This formulation suggests that the consumer maximizes utility when the ratio of marginal utility to price is equalized for all commodities. In addition, it is possible to interpret λ in this equation as the *marginal utility of money* when utility is maximized.

6-3b A Cobb-Douglas Utility Function

Cobb-Douglas functions, used most frequently to represent production relationships, are also often used as specific forms for utility analysis. One important application is to derive demand curves for goods based on a Cobb-Douglas function. Suppose the utility function for economics classes and skiing trips is given by Equation 6-14:

$$U = C^{\alpha}S^{1-\alpha} \qquad (6\text{-}14)$$

where $0 < \alpha < 1$. With this specification, many of the familiar propositions of utility analysis apply: Each good is subject to diminishing marginal utility, the indifference curves for the function are downward sloping, and they are convex. Assuming again that the budget constraint is

$$I = P_C C + P_S S$$

and utility maximization is the objective of the consumer, the Lagrangian expression is shown in Equation 6-15:

$$L = C^{\alpha}S^{1-\alpha} - \lambda(P_C C + P_S S - I) \qquad (6\text{-}15)$$

Finding the partial derivatives and setting them equal to zero yields Equations 6-16, 6-17, and 6-18:

$$\partial L / \partial C = \alpha C^{\alpha-1}S^{1-\alpha} - \lambda P_C = 0 \qquad (6\text{-}16)$$

$$\partial L / \partial S = (1-\alpha)C^{\alpha}S^{-\alpha} - \lambda P_S = 0 \qquad (6\text{-}17)$$

$$\partial L / \partial \lambda = I - P_C C - P_S S = 0 \qquad (6\text{-}18)$$

Suppose we solve Equation 6-16 for C and Equation 6-17 for S:

$$C = \alpha C^{\alpha}S^{1-\alpha} / \lambda P_c \qquad (6\text{-}16')$$

$$S = (1-\alpha)C^{\alpha}S^{1-\alpha} / \lambda P_S \qquad (6\text{-}17')$$

To eliminate λ from the equations, substitute Equations 6-16′ and Equation 6-17′ into Equation 6-18 and solve for λ as shown in Equation 6-19:

$$\lambda = C^{\alpha}S^{1-\alpha} / I \qquad (6\text{-}19)$$

Finally substitute the expression for λ from Equation 6-19 into Equation 6-16′ and Equation 6-17′ to obtain Equation 6-20:

$$C = \alpha I / P_C \qquad (6\text{-}20)$$

and Equation 6-21:

$$S = (1-\alpha) I / P_S \qquad (6\text{-}21)$$

Equations 6-20 and 6-21 are the *generalized* demand functions[1] for economics classes (C) and skiing trips (S). These demand functions are downward sloping and have constant price elasticity of demand equal to unity. That the demand curves slope downward is obvious from the observation that the numerator of each function is a constant and the price of the good is in the denominator. The equation is also a rectangular hyperbola since total expenditure on classes, $P_C \cdot C$ equals αI, and αI, the product of two constants, must also be a constant. If total expenditure is constant for any values of P and C that satisfy Equation 6-20, price elasticity of demand must equal one ($\eta = 1$).

It is also possible to derive the income consumption curves from the first-order conditions for utility maximization. Solving Equations 6-16 and 6-17 for λ yields Equation 6-22:

1. The term *generalized* is used to differentiate these demand functions from *compensated* demand functions, in which the level of utility is held constant when price changes.

$$\lambda = \frac{\alpha C^{\alpha-1}S^{1-\alpha}}{P_C} = \frac{(1-\alpha)C^{\alpha}S^{-\alpha}}{P_S} \qquad (6\text{-}22)$$

Equation 6-212may be solved for either S or C to produce an income consumption curve. Choosing to solve for C, the income consumption curve (line) is shown in Equation 6-23:

$$C = \frac{\alpha P_S}{(1-\alpha)P_C} \bullet S \qquad (6\text{-}23)$$

which is linear because α, P_C, and P_S are constants. Equation 6-23 shows that the income consumption curve for the linearly homogeneous utility function is a straight line emanating from the origin. The economics of this result is that the two goods would be consumed in the same *ratio* for differing levels of income. This type of situation is depicted in Figure 6-2. The tangency positions of the indifference curves and the different budget lines (lines AB, DF, and GH) lie on the straight-line income consumption curve (ICC). In fact, the Cobb-Douglas function will have a linear income consumption curve even if the exponents do not sum to one; that is, for equations that are homogeneous of degrees other than one.[2] For the more general case, suppose the utility function is as shown in Equation 6-24:

$$U = C^{\alpha}S^{\beta} \qquad (6\text{-}24)$$

The income consumption curve can be shown to be

$$C = \frac{\alpha P_S}{\beta P_C} \bullet S$$

which is again linear and positively sloped for values of α and β greater than zero.

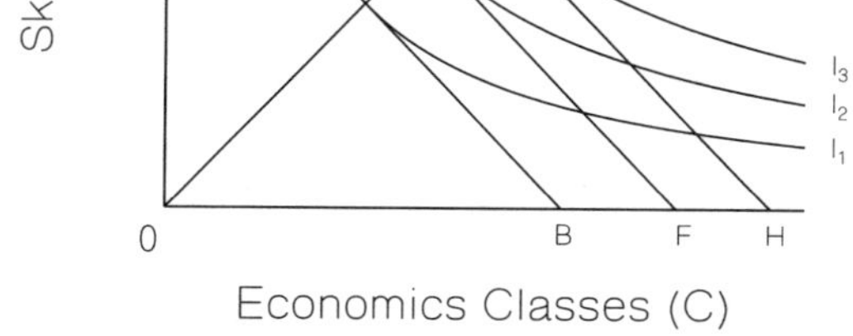

Figure 6-2
Income consumption curve.

2. In fact, any homogeneous utility (or production function) can result in linear income consumption curves (or expansion paths).

The student of microeconomics should note that the income consumption curve implied by these Cobb-Douglas utility functions would rule out "Engel effects" for the two goods in question (the idea that the proportion of income spent on some goods will fall or rise as income rises). The student should also recognize that the entire preceding analysis could have been applied in a production context. The utility function could have been a production function for, say, umbrellas (U) as a function of the inputs, steel (S) and canvas (C). The demand functions are in this case input demands and a linear *expansion path* is the corresponding production concept to the income consumption curve. When the production expansion path is linear, the ratios of the inputs are always the same for differing levels of input expenditure in equilibrium.

6-4 Imperfect Competition and Taxation

In Chapter 2, "Microeconomic Applications of Equations and Graphs," we considered excise taxation in competitive markets. We now consider the case of imperfect competition and taxation. Suppose The Heavy Duty Squirt Gun Company owns the U.S. patent for double-barreled Demon Drencher squirt guns. The total revenue and total cost functions are shown in Equations 6-25 and 6-26:

$$\text{Total Revenue} = TR = 50Q - 2Q^2 \tag{6-25}$$

$$\text{Total Cost} = TC = 10Q \tag{6-26}$$

where Q is millions of squirt guns per month and costs and revenues are in dollars. The profit (π) function is TR – TC (see Equation 6-27):

$$\pi = 50Q - 2Q^2 - 10Q \tag{6-27}$$

Assuming that the firm seeks to maximize profit, the profit maximizing output is found by differentiating Equation 6-27 with respect to Q and setting the result equal to zero, as shown in Equation 6-28.

$$d\pi/dQ = 50 - 4Q - 10 = 0 \tag{6-28}$$

Solving Equation 6-28 for Q, Q = 10 million squirt guns per month. Recognize that marginal revenue is 50 – 4Q and marginal cost is 10, so Equation 6-28 requires MR = MC. To find the price of a squirt gun, remember that the demand curve is average revenue = price = total revenue divided by quantity, as shown in Equation 6-29:

$$P = TR/Q = (50Q - 2Q^2)/Q = 50 - 2Q \tag{6-29}$$

So when Q = 10, P = \$30 per squirt gun. Profit from Equation 6-27 is

$$\pi = 50(10) - 2(10)^2 - 10(10) = \$200 \text{ (million)}$$

or \$200,000,000 dollars per month.

Now suppose that the U.S. federal government, in a period of fiscal crisis and with a zeal to discourage the use of squirt guns, decides to impose an excise tax on Demon Drencher squirt guns. The tax is to be t dollars per gun. The government, more interested in tax revenues than in discouraging squirt gun use, decides to set the tax rate so as to maximize tax receipts. The objective function for the government is the tax revenue equation shown in Equation 6-30:

$$T = tQ_e \tag{6-30}$$

where Q_e is the *equilibrium quantity*, the quantity at which the firm maximizes profit after the tax is imposed. The total costs of the firm, which must remit the tax to the city, now include the amount of the excise tax. Let TC_t represent total costs including the tax, as shown in Equation 6-31:

$$TC_t = TC + tQ = 10Q + tQ \tag{6-31}$$

The profit function is shown in Equation 6-32:

$$\pi = 50Q - 2Q^2 - 10Q - tQ \tag{6-32}$$

The maximum profit for the firm is found where the derivative of Equation 6-32 equals zero:

$$d\pi/dQ = 50 - 4Q - 10 - t = 0$$

Therefore:

$$Q_e = 10 - (1/4)t$$

Substituting this equilibrium quantity into Equation 6-30 gives us Equation 6-33:

$$T = 10t - (1/4)t^2 \tag{6-33}$$

To maximize tax revenues, differentiate Equation 6-33 with respect to t, set the result equal to zero, and solve for t:

$$dT/dt = 10 - (1/2)t = 0$$

Thus $t = 20$, or the tax that maximizes revenues for the city is \$20 per squirt gun. (Since $d^2T/dt^2 = -1/2 < 0$, we can be sure that $t = 20$ *maximizes* T.) The actual level of tax receipts to the city are given by substituting into Equation 6-33:

$$T = 10(20) - (1/4)20^2 = 100$$

or 100 million dollars (\$100,000,000). The \$100,000,000 in tax revenues could also have been computed as the product of the tax (\$20 per squirt gun) and the after-tax equilibrium quantity, which we will now show to be 5 million squirt guns per month.

After the tax is imposed, Equation 6-32 becomes Equation 6-32′:

$$\pi = 50Q - 2Q^2 - 10Q - 20Q \tag{6-32′}$$

where the last term on the right-hand side is the "tax" component of total costs (terms could be combined). Differentiating Equation 6-32′ and setting the result equal to zero in order to find the new equilibrium quantity yields

$$d\pi/dQ = 50 - 4Q - 10 - 20 = 0$$

Thus Q = 5, and from Equation 6-32′ profit is $50 million dollars ($50,000,000) per month. From Equation 6-29 the new price is

$$P = 50 - 2Q = 50 - 2(5) = 40$$

or $40 per squirt gun, so only a portion (one half) of the tax is passed on to the consumer.

6-5 A Duopoly Model

The models of *duopoly* (two firms make up the industry) considered in microeconomics typically include the Cournot duopoly model. This model is a special case of the more general *Nash equilibria* approach to noncooperative games. The simplest approach to the Cournot duopoly model assumes the following:

- Demand curves are linear.
- The good is homogeneous.
- Marginal cost is zero.
- Each firm makes its output decision assuming the other firm's output is fixed at its current level.

Typically the Cournot model begins with one firm operating as a monopolist and then allowing the other firm to enter the market. Suppose we have the linear market demand curve pictured in Figure 6-3, which has the vertical (price) intercept at point a and the horizontal (quantity) intercept at point b. The slope of the demand curve is equal to –a/b, since we can measure slope between any two points on a linear demand curve, including points a and b. The marginal revenue (MR) curve has the same vertical intercept as the demand curve and twice the slope. If the commodity is spring water, the market demand curve may be written as in Equation 6-34:

$$P_W = a - (a/b)Q \qquad (6\text{-}34)$$

where P_W is the price of spring water and the total quantity offered (Q) is the sum of the outputs of the two firms in the market. Let q_1 and q_2 represent the individual outputs of firms one and two, respectively. Equation 6-34 may be rewritten as Equation 6-34′:

$$P_W = a - (a/b)(q_1 + q_2) \qquad (6\text{-}34')$$

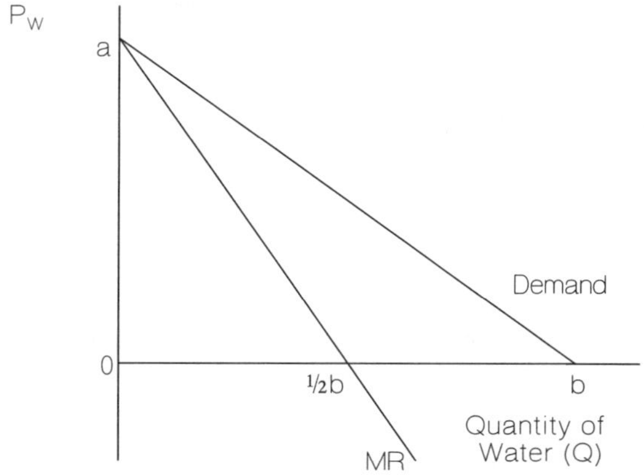

Figure 6-3
Spring water duopoly.

6-5a Reaction Functions

Since there are no costs, the profit function for firm 1 is the same as the total revenue function ($P_W \cdot q_1$) for firm 1, as shown in Equation 6-35:

$$\pi_1 = [a - (a/b)(q_1 + q_2)]q_1 = aq_1 - (a/b)(q_1^2 + q_1q_2) \quad (6\text{-}35)$$

For maximum profit for firm 1, differentiate Equation 6-35 with respect to q_1 and set the result equal to zero as in Equation 6-36:

$$d\pi_1/dq_1 = a - 2(a/b)q_1 - (a/b)q_2 = 0 \quad (6\text{-}36)$$

Solving Equation 6-36 for q_1 yields Equation 6-37:

$$q_1 = (\tfrac{1}{2})(b - q_2) \quad (6\text{-}37)$$

Equation 6-37 is known as the *reaction function* for firm 1, since it determines how much output firm 1 will produce (q_1) as a function of the output of firm 2 (q_2).

Similarly, the profit function for firm 2 is shown in Equation 6-38:

$$\pi_2 = [a - (a/b)(q_1 + q_2)]q_2 = aq_2 - (a/b)(q_2^2 + q_1q_2) \quad (6\text{-}38)$$

and the first-order condition is shown in Equation 6-39:

$$d\pi_2/dq_2 = a - 2(a/b)q_2 - (a/b)q_1 = 0 \quad (6\text{-}39)$$

Solving Equation 6-39 for q_2 gives us Equation 6-40

$$q_2 = (\tfrac{1}{2})(b - q_1) \quad (6\text{-}40)$$

The reaction functions for each firm are based on the output for the other firm. Therefore, we can substitute the equation for q_1 (Equation 6-37) into the equation for q_2 (Equation 6-40) to get Equation 6-41:

$$q_2 = (\tfrac{1}{2})[b - (\tfrac{1}{2})(b - q_2)] = (\tfrac{1}{2})b - (\tfrac{1}{4})b + (\tfrac{1}{4})q_2 \quad (6\text{-}41)$$

Solving Equation 6-41 for q_2 yields Equation 6-42:

$$q_2 = (1/3)b \tag{6-42}$$

Substitute Equation 6-42 into Equation 6-37 to find q_1 in Equation 6-43:

$$q_1 = (1/2)[b - (1/3)b] = (1/3)b \tag{6-43}$$

Equations 6-42 and 6-43 show that, in equilibrium, each firm produces an output of (⅓)b, so equilibrium total output is (⅔)b; that is, $q_1 + q_2 = Q = (2/3)b$, and the equilibrium market price (⅓) a can be found by substituting (⅔)b into Equation 6-34.

Figure 6-4 shows the two reaction functions, where the vertical axis is the output of firm 2, q_2, and the horizontal axis measures the output of firm 1, q_1. R_1 is the reaction function for firm 1 and R_2 is the reaction function for firm 2. The equilibrium is found at the intersection of the two reaction functions, where $q_1 = (1/3)b$ along the horizontal axis and $q_2 = (1/3)b$ along the vertical axis. The process of convergence to the equilibrium outputs is straightforward. Consider Figure 6-5, where firm 1 enters the market first. Since the output for firm 2 is zero, the output for firm 1, read off R_1, is $q_{1'}$. The reaction of firm 2 is found on R_2 directly above $q_{1'}$, hence firm 2 produces $q_{2'}$. With the output of firm 2 now at $q_{2'}$, firm 1 will react with an output of $q_{1''}$ (read across from $q_{2'}$ to R_1 and down to $q_{1''}$. The reaction of firm 2 reaction is now to produce $q_{2''}$, and so on. This iterative process will eventually reduce the output of firm 1 to the equilibrium level and raise the output of firm 2 to the equilibrium level, as indicated by the arrows. Finally, each firm will be in equilibrium at the outputs indicated at the intersection of their reaction functions, with each firm producing (⅓)b.

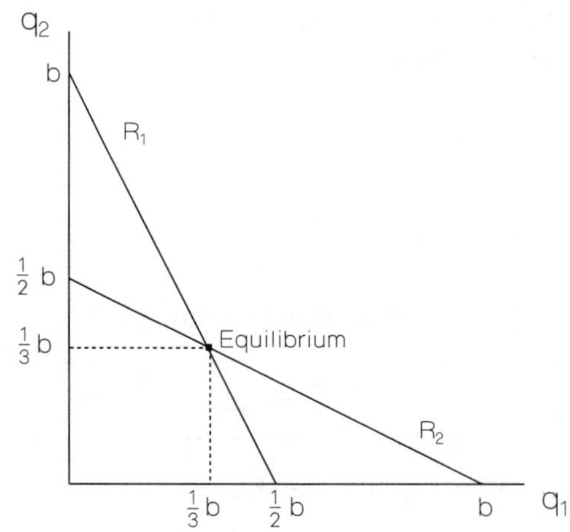

Figure 6-4
Cournot duopoly reaction functions.

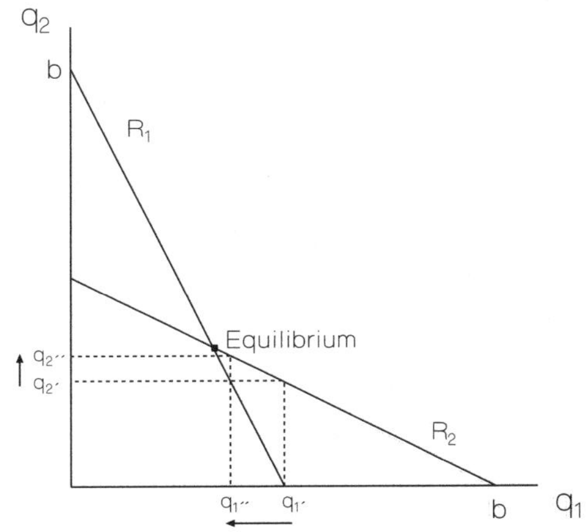

Figure 6-5
Convergence based on the reaction functions.

6-5b Cournot, Monopoly, and Competition

Although the Cournot model is often criticized as being naïve, especially in its assumptions, it is intuitively appealing when compared to the models of monopoly and perfect competition. Consider again Figure 6-3, where the monopoly output can be found by setting marginal cost (which is zero) equal to marginal revenue. The monopolist would produce an output of ($\frac{1}{2}$)b, and the corresponding price would be ($\frac{1}{2}$)a. Notice from either reaction function (Equation 6-37 or 6-40) that if the output of the "other" firm is zero, the equilibrium output is indeed equal to the monopoly output, which is the expected result with only one firm in the industry. Output for the duopoly equilibrium is ($\frac{2}{3}$)b, more than the monopoly output, and price ($\frac{1}{3}$)a is also lower than the monopoly price. The competitive output is found where marginal cost equals price (MC = P), or an output of b, where P = 0. The Cournot duopoly output and price equilibrium values fit nicely between the monopoly and competitive extremes.

As we have just noted, the Cournot model predicts a price and an output that falls between monopoly and competition. We also saw that monopoly is a special case of the Cournot model where the "other" firm's output is zero. It is also possible to show that the competitive equilibrium would be predicted by extending the number of firms to a large number (n) under the reaction functions approach proposed by Cournot. To begin, suppose there are three firms, with the first two offering ($\frac{1}{4}$)b. The remaining firm would maximize profits over the remaining output (and demand) according to the following equation:

$$q_3 = \tfrac{1}{2}[b - (\tfrac{1}{4})b - (\tfrac{1}{4})b] = (\tfrac{1}{4})b$$

Since firms 1 and 2 respond with the same output,

$$q_1 = q_2 = \tfrac{1}{2}[b - (\tfrac{1}{4})b - (\tfrac{1}{4})b] = (\tfrac{1}{4})b$$

we have an equilibrium market output of ($\frac{3}{4}$)b , which is the sum $q_1 + q_2 + q_3$. Similarly, nine firms would each offer (1/10)b and total output would equal (9/10)b. As n firms are allowed to enter the market, the output becomes the competitive output, b. Put simply, the Cournot model produces the competitive results for a large number of firms.

6-6 Summary

This chapter presented a number of common applications of the mathematical tools for finding maxima and minima. Many other applications are possible. The important thing for the student to learn from these applications is how to go about the business of applying the techniques from Chapter 5 to the wide variety of problems that arise in the study of microeconomics. The problems at the end of this chapter and the many applications from your microeconomics textbook will also aid the student in appreciating the use of mathematics, and especially optimization, as it applies to the subject matter of microeconomic theory.

Problems

1. A firm in the perfectly competitive tire industry has the following total cost and total revenue functions:

$$TC = 50 + 100q - 6q^2 + \tfrac{1}{3}q^3$$
$$TR = 89q$$

where TC is total cost, TR is total revenue, and q is the output of the firm in hundreds of tires per month.

(a) Form the profit function and find the output at which profit is maximized. There will be two solution values, so check the second-order condition for a maximum.
(b) Find the levels of cost, revenue, and profit at the profit maximizing output.

Now suppose the price to the firm falls to $68, meaning that total revenue is now

$$TR = 68q$$

(c) Form the profit function and find the output at which profit is maximized. There will be two solution values, so check the second-order condition for a maximum.
(d) Find the levels of cost, revenue, and profit at the profit maximizing output.
(e) You have found the mathematical maximum for the profit function. Is your answer also an *economic* solution? Why or why not?

2. The production function for ballpoint pens is given by the Cobb-Douglas function:

$$Q = K^{.5}L^{.5}$$

where Q is output per month and K and L are capital and labor inputs, respectively. The price of labor is $20 per unit, the price of capital is $10 per unit, and the firm has $10,000 to spend on inputs each month.

(a) Write the equation for the iso-cost (budget) line.
(b) Write the Lagrangian expression for maximizing output subject to the isocost constraint.
(c) Find the optimal amounts of capital and labor to be employed and the level of output for those optimal levels.

3. Consider again the production function in Problem 2. Suppose the iso-cost line is written generally as

$$R = rK + wL$$

where R = expenditure on inputs, r is the payment to capital (rent), and w is the payment to labor (wages).

(a) Write the Lagrangian function for maximizing output subject to this generalized iso-cost line.
(b) Following the procedures outlined in the chapter (Equations 6-18 through 6-21), find the demand functions for the inputs, capital, and labor.

Recognize that these demand functions do not have the price of the output as an argument in the factor demand equation. That is only because we have implicitly assumed the price of output to be 1. Profit, which is what the firm is assumed to maximize, is total revenue minus total cost. Total revenue with a price level of one is simply the production function,

$$Q = K^{.5}L^{.5}$$

Total cost is

$$rK + wL$$

(c) Could you have found the same results as above by maximizing profit? Try it.

4. A production function is given by

$$Q = 120L^2K^2 - L^3K^3$$

If K is fixed at 10, find the level of L that maximizes output.

5. The production of preprinted address labels at a particular plant of the IRS is characterized by the following production function:

$$Q = (30L - L^2)(100K - K^2)$$

where Q is the number of labels produced per month, L is the number of workers employed, and K is the number of printers available for printing. Notice that output is positive for $0 < L < 30$ and $0 < K < 100$. Find the maximum monthly output that can be produced at this plant.

6. The (empty) whiskey barrel market in Prohibition, Kansas is perfectly competitive with the *quarterly* demand and supply equations:

$$P = 120 - 3Q_d$$
$$P = Q_s$$

where P is in dollars per barrel and Q is in hundreds of barrels per quarter year.

The city decides to levy a per-unit tax on the suppliers of these barrels. Mayor Dogooder calls you in as a consultant to determine the level at which the tax should be set if the objective is to maximize tax receipts. Determine the tax per barrel and the amount of tax collected each quarter.

7. The Cournot duopoly model applies to the market for warm nuclear wastewater. The demand curve for the water is given by

$$P = 200 - 2Q$$

where P is price in cents per bottle and Q is hundreds of bottles per month.

(a) Find the Cournot reaction functions for the two firms.
(b) Find the Cournot equilibrium price and the quantity for each firm and for the market.
(c) Compare the Cournot results in part b with the results from monopoly equilibrium and competitive equilibrium for the same market demand curve.

Now assume that each Cournot duopolist has constant marginal costs of 40¢ per bottle.

(d) Find the Cournot reaction functions for the two firms under the assumption of MC = 40¢.
(e) Find the Cournot equilibrium price and the quantity for each firm and for the market.
(f) Compare the Cournot results in part e with the results from monopoly equilibrium and competitive equilibrium for the same market demand curve.

8. Greedy University acts as a profit-maximizing discriminating monopolist in the "sales" of student positions. That is, the University separates the demands of in-state students and out-of-state students in order to charge different prices to each group in an attempt to maximize profit (minimize losses). The demand curves of each group are given as

$$P_1 = 20000 - 3q_1$$

$$P_2 = 15000 - q_2$$

where P is price in thousands of dollars per year, and the subscripts 1 and 2 refer to out-of-state and in-state students, respectively. The marginal cost of each student to Greedy U is constant at $8,000 per student and fixed costs are $24 million per year. The total cost function is then

$$TC = 24{,}000{,}000 + 8000(q_1 + q_2)$$

(a) Write the profit function (π) for Greedy University.
(b) Find the values of q_1 and q_2 that will produce a maximum for the profit function.
(c) What prices will be charged for each group?
(d) Find the level of profit for Greedy.
(e) Finally, compute price elasticity of demand for each group for the price Greedy U charges each group. Explain how price elasticity determines which price is higher.

9. Garth and Wayne have $38 to spend each week on doughnuts from Stan Mikita's and posters of their favorite movie star. Doughnuts (D) at Stan Mikita's sell for 50 cents each, and posters (P) sell for two dollars each. Furthermore, Garth and Wayne share the utility function:

$$U = 10D + 80P - D^2 - 2P^2$$

(a) Write the Lagrangian expression for maximizing U with respect to the budget constraint.
(b) Determine the amounts of doughnuts and posters that will maximize Wayne and Garth's utility given their budget constraint.
(c) Check second-order conditions to make sure that you have found a maximum.

Appendix

Solutions to Problems

Chapter 1

1. (a)

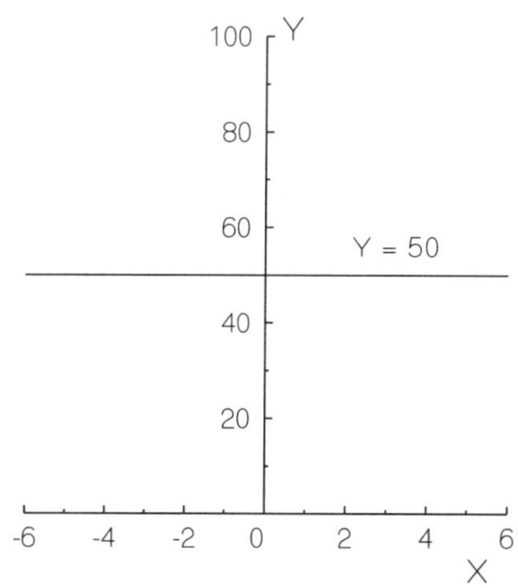

(b)

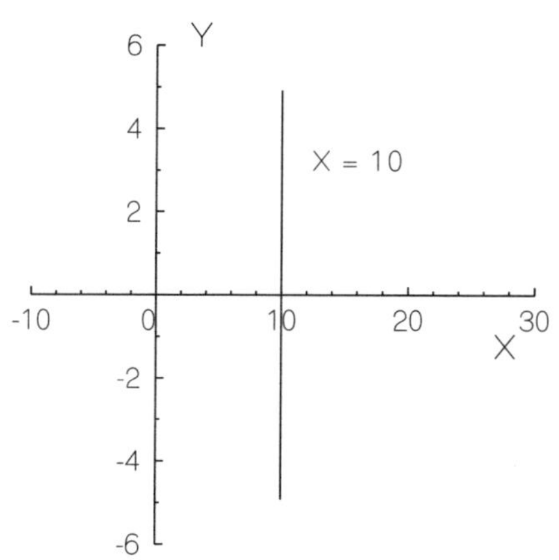

(c)

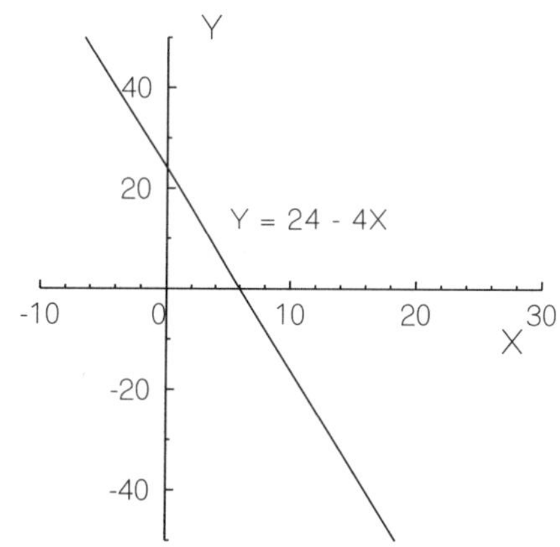

(d)

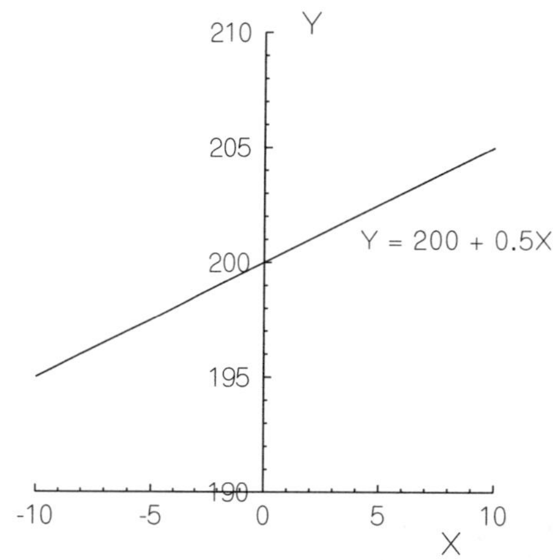

(e)

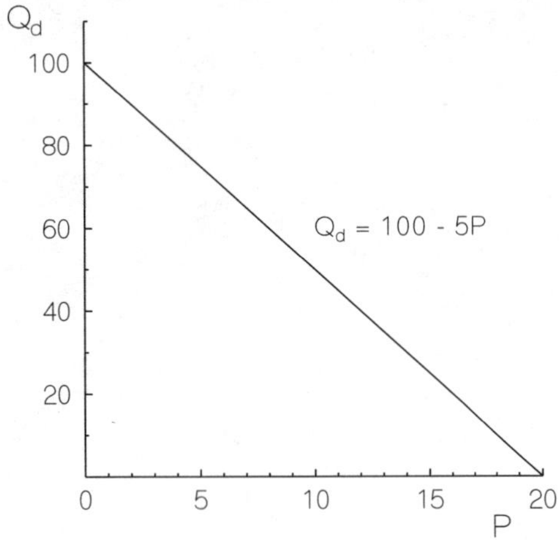

(f)

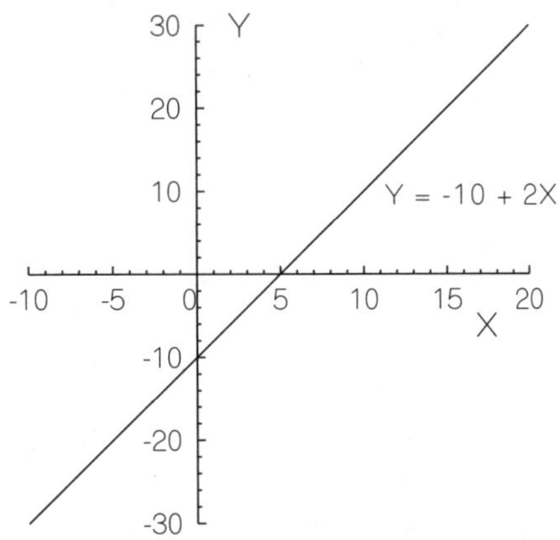

2. (a) 0
   (b) ∞ or undefined
   (c) –4
   (d) +0.5
   (e) –5
   (f) +2

3. Solve the following quadratics (set y = 0) by factoring or by the quadratic formula.

   (a) x = –4, x = 3
   (b) x = 5, x = 2
   (c) x = 4, x = –5/2
   (d) x = 1.5344..., x = –1.2219...

4. (a) constant
   (b) constant
   (c) straight line
   (d) straight line
   (e) quadratic
   (f) cubic
   (g) cubic
   (h) hyperbola
   (i) hyperbola
   (j) exponential
   (k) exponential

5. (a)

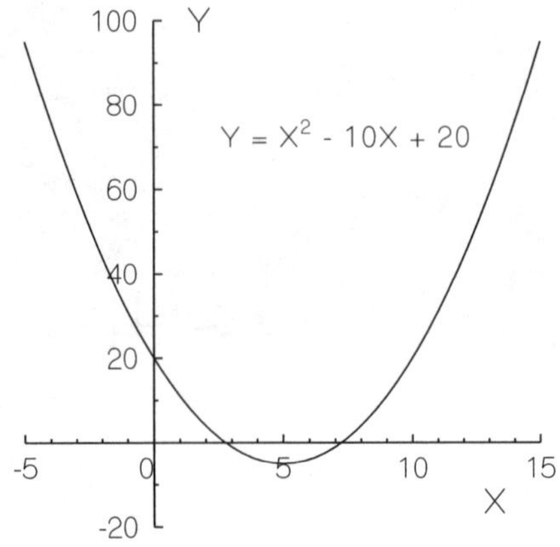

(b)

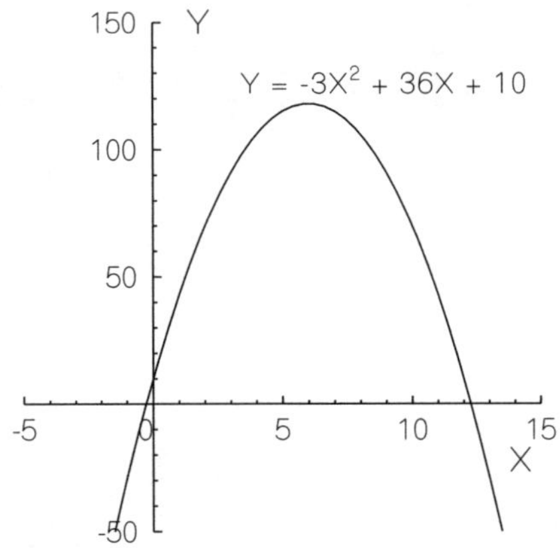

(c)

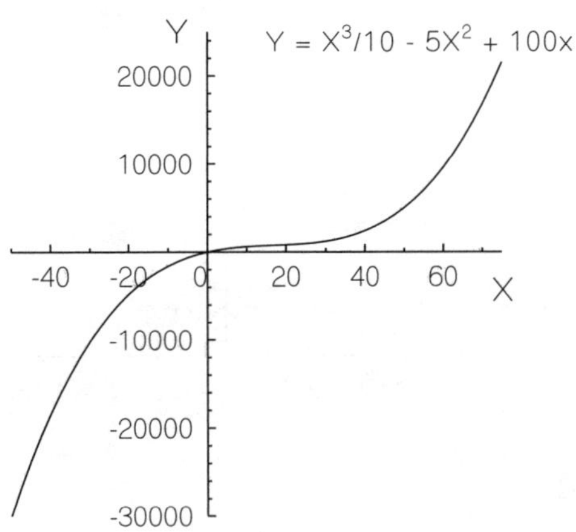

(d)

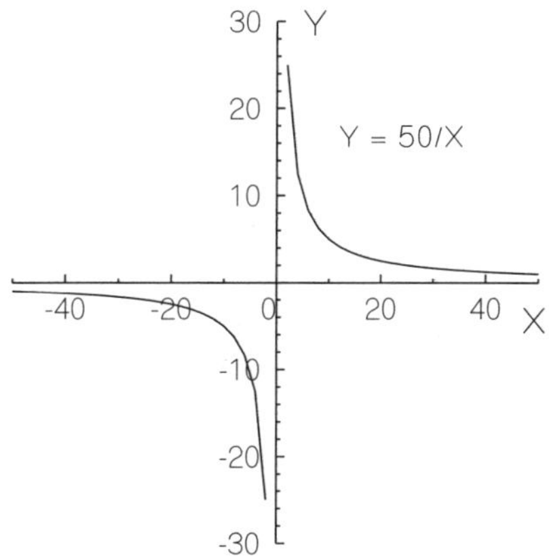

(e)

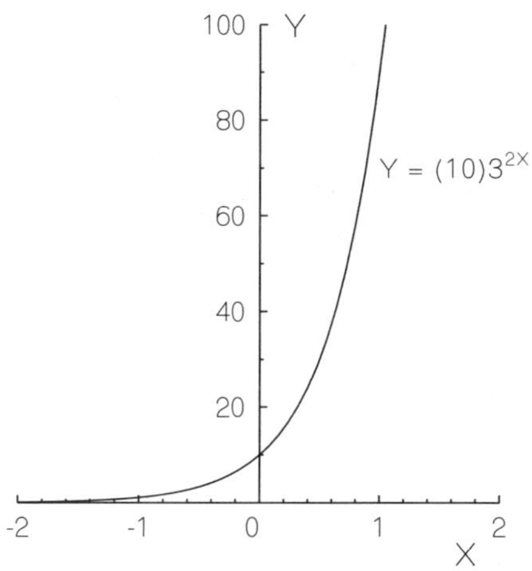

(f)

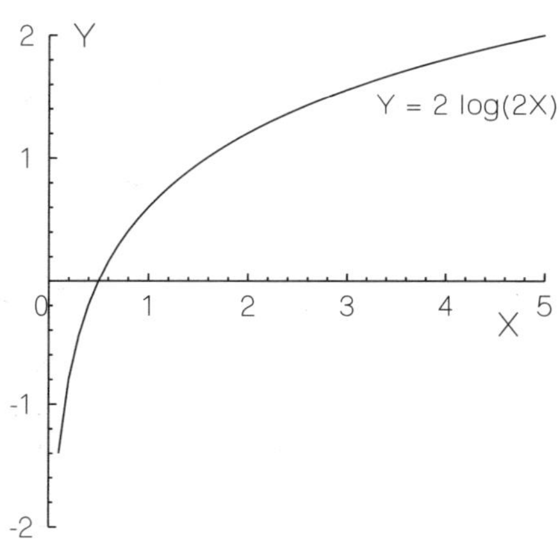

Chapter 2

1. (a) $Q_d = 12/P$ or $Q_d = 12P^{-1}$.
   (b) $Q_d = 6$ when $P = 2$ and $Q_d = 3$ when $P = 4$.
   (c) Since \$12 is spent regardless of price, $\eta = 1$ by definition. Also, if we use the solutions from part b of this question and modify Equation 2-6 in this chapter so that P and Q are the averages of the two prices and two quantities respectively, we can directly compute the following:

   $\eta = -(\Delta Q/\Delta P)(P/Q) = -(-3/2)(3/4.5) = 1$

   This modified formula is known as the *arc price elasticity of demand formula.* Finally, if the form of the demand curve can be written as $Q_d = aP^{-\eta}$, the value of the exponent is the *coefficient of price elasticity of demand.*

2. (a) Set $Q_d = Q_s$, $12/P = P$, $P^2 = 12$, so $P = \sqrt{12} = \pm \$3.4641$. The positive root makes sense so $P = \$3.4641$. If $P = \$3.4641$, $Q = 3.4641$ million pounds.
   (b) $P - 4 = Q_s$.
   (c) $12/P = P - 4$, so $P^2 - 4P - 12 = 0$. The solution values are $P = \$6$ or $P = \$-2$. The correct choice is $P = \$6$. From either the demand or the supply curve, $Q = 2$.
   (d) The buyer now pays \$2.54 more per pound and the seller receives \$1.46 less per pound after paying the tax.
   (e) $Q_d = 12/6 = 2$ or 1.4641 fewer pounds per month.

3. (a) FC = 10.
   (b) $ATC = TC/q = 10/q + 10 - 5q + q^2$
   (c) $AVC = 10 - 5q + q^2$
   (d) $10 - 10q + 3q^2 = 10 - 5q + q^2$
   $q = 2.5$ (thousands), therefore $AVC = 10 - 5(2.5) + (2.5)^2 = 3.75$ (dollars per watch)

4. (a) $3q^2 - 10q + 10 = 20$
   $3q^2 - 10q - 10 = 0$
   $q = 4.1387$, $q = -0.8054$ (Only $q = 4.1387$ makes economic sense.)
   (b) TC = 36.636, TR = 82.774, so π (profit) = 46.138 (thousands of dollars per period)

5. (a) 1000 = 10CD + 20M or CD = 100 – 2M or M = 50 – ½CD.
   (b) CD = 100 – 2(25) = 50.
   (c) 750 = 10CD + 10M or CD = 75 – M.
   (d) If M = 25, CD = 75 – 25 = 50.
   (e) The tangency position in the recession is on a higher indifference curve.

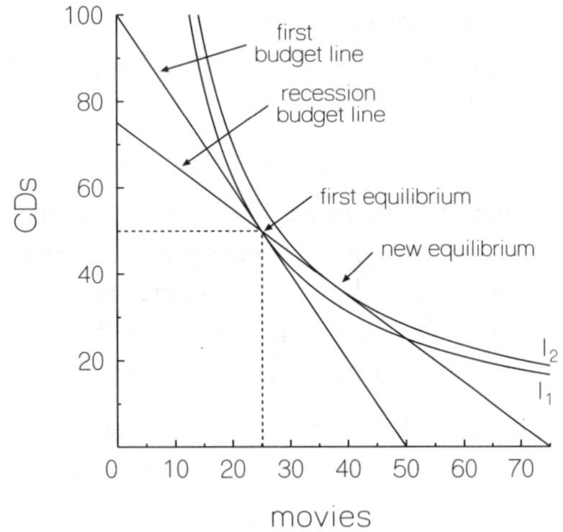

6. $10e^{2Q} = 25000e^{-.5Q}$
$\ln 10 + 2Q \ln e = \ln 25000 - .5Q \ln e$
$\ln 10 + 2Q = \ln 25000 - .5Q$
$2.5Q = \ln 25000 - \ln 10$
$Q = 3.1296$ (approximately 313 units per month)
$P = 10e^{2(3.1296)} = 5{,}228$ (dollars per unit)

Chapter 3

1. (a) $dy/dx = 2$
(b) $dy/dx = 0$
(c) $dy/dx = 6x$
(d) $dy/dx = 2x(2x) + (x^2 + 3)2 = 6x^2 + 6$
(e) $dy/dx = (3x^2 - x^3)(2 + 20x^4) + (2x + 4x^5)(6x - 3x^2) = -32x^7 + 84x^6 - 8x^3 + 18x^2$
(f) $dy/dx = 12x + 20$
(g) $\dfrac{dy}{dx} = \dfrac{2x(6 + 6x) - (6x + 3x^2)(2)}{4x^2} = \dfrac{3}{2}$
(h) $\dfrac{dy}{dx} = \dfrac{(x - 3)(4x^3 - 6x) - (x^4 + 3x^2)(1)}{(x - 3)^2} = \dfrac{3x^4 - 12x^3 - 3x^2 + 18x}{x^2 - 6x + 9}$
(i) $\dfrac{dy}{dx} = \dfrac{dy}{du} \cdot \dfrac{du}{dx} = 2(12x + 3) = 24x + 6$
(j) $\dfrac{dy}{dx} = \dfrac{dy}{du} \cdot \dfrac{du}{dx} = 4u(-4x) = -16ux = -16x(6 - 2x^2) = 32x^3 - 96x$
(k) $dy/dx = 4(3x^2 - 2x^3 - 10)^3(6x - 6x^2) = (24x - 24x^2)(3x^2 - 2x^3 - 10)^3$
(l) $\dfrac{dy}{dx} = \dfrac{1}{4x^2 + x} \cdot (8x + 1) = \dfrac{8x + 1}{x(4x + 1)}$
(m)
$$\frac{dy}{dx} = 2x\left(\frac{1}{4x^2 + 3x}\right) \cdot (8x + 3) + 2\ln(4x^2 + 3x) = \frac{16x + 6}{4x + 3} + 2\ln(4x^2 + 3x)$$
(n) $\dfrac{dy}{dx} = 2^{(x^2 - 3x + 2)} \cdot (\ln 2)(2x - 3)$
(o) $dy/dx = 2(e^{2x})2 = 4e^{2x}$
(p) $dy/dx = 3x(e^{2x+1})2 + 3e^{2x+1} = (6x + 3)e^{2x+1}$

2. (a) $4x - 12y^3(dy/dx) + 4[2xy(dy/dx) + y^2] = 0$, and solving: $dy/dx = (-y^2 - x)/(2xy - 3y^3)$
(b) $3[2xy^2 + 2x^2y(dy/dx)] + 2[y^2 + 2xy(dy/dx)] - 10x + 1/x$
$(dy/dx)(6x^2y + 4xy) = -6xy^2 - 2y^2 + 10x - 1/x$
$\dfrac{dy}{dx} = \dfrac{-6xy^2 - 2y^2 + 10x - 1/x}{(6x^2y + 4xy)}$

3. (a) $\partial z/\partial x = 8x^3 - 2y$
(b) $\partial z/\partial y = 6y - 2x + 3$

4. (a) $\partial y/\partial u = (3u^2 + v)0 + (2v + 5)6u = 12uv + 30u$
(b) $\partial y/\partial v = (3u^2 + v)2 + (2v + 5)1 = 6u^2 + 4v + 5$

Alternatively, the original expression could be multiplied out, and that expression differentiated.

5. (a) $dz = (4xy - y)dx + (2x^2 - x)dy$
(b) $dz = (10x + 4y^2)dx + (-6y + 8xy)dy$

6. (a) $\dfrac{dy}{dz} = \dfrac{\partial y}{\partial x}\dfrac{dx}{dz} + \dfrac{\partial y}{\partial z} = (3 + 2z)(9z^2) + 2x - 2z = 18z^3 + 27z^2 - 2z + 2x$
(b) $\dfrac{dy}{dz} = \dfrac{\partial y}{\partial x}\dfrac{dx}{dz} + \dfrac{\partial y}{\partial z} = (1 - z)(-1) - x + 6z = 7z - x - 1$

7. (a) $\dfrac{du}{dx} = \dfrac{\partial u}{\partial y}\dfrac{dy}{dx} + \dfrac{\partial u}{\partial x} = .5x^{.5}y^{-.5}(-2) + .5x^{-.5}y^{.5} = -\dfrac{x^{.5}}{y^{.5}} + \dfrac{.5y^{.5}}{x^{.5}}$
(b) $\dfrac{du}{dx} = \dfrac{\partial u}{\partial y}\dfrac{dy}{dx} + \dfrac{\partial u}{\partial x} = (x + 4y)(-1) + 2x + y = x - 3y$

Chapter 4

1. (a) $MC = d(TC)/dq = 30q^2$
   (b) $ATC = TC/q = 10q^2 + 160/q$
   (c) $MC = ATC$
   $30q^2 = 10q^2 + 160/q$
   $20q^2 = 160/q$
   $20q^3 = 160$
   $q^3 = 8$, $q = 2$ (two hundred bags per week)

   First, ATC is "U" shaped. Second, if the marginal is less than the average, the average is declining; if the marginal exceeds the average, the average is increasing. Therefore, the marginal intersects the average at its minimum point.

   (d) $ATC = 10(2^2) + 160/2 = 120$ (120 dollars per hundred bags or \$1.20 per bag)

2. (a) $$MP_L = \frac{\partial Q}{\partial L} = 7.5L^{-.25}K^{.25} = 7.5\left(\frac{K}{L}\right)^{.25}$$

   (b) $$MP_K = \frac{\partial Q}{\partial K} = 2.5L^{.75}K^{-.75} = 2.5\left(\frac{L}{K}\right)^{.75}$$

   (c) $$AP_L = \frac{Q}{L} = \frac{10L^{.75}K^{.25}}{L} = 10\left(\frac{K}{L}\right)^{.25}$$

   $$AP_K = \frac{Q}{K} = \frac{10L^{.75}K^{.25}}{K} = 10\left(\frac{L}{K}\right)^{.75}$$

   (d) $Q = 10L^{.75}K^{.25} = Q = 10(80^{.75})(50^{.25}) = 711.31$ (dozens of balls per month)
   From Euler's Theorem, $Q = L(MP_L) + K(MP_K)$:

   $$Q = L\frac{\partial Q}{\partial L} + K\frac{\partial Q}{\partial K} = (80)(7.5)\left(\frac{50}{80}\right)^{.25} + (50)(2.5)\left(\frac{80}{50}\right)^{.75} = 711.31$$

3. (a) Yes, the exponents sum to 1 (.75 + .25 = 1).
   (b) They are all homogeneous of degree zero. This means that the marginal and average products do not change if L and K are changed by the same proportion. In other words, the marginal and average products depend only on the ratios of labor and capital when the equations are homogeneous of degree zero.

4. (a) 0.9
   (b) $MP_L = \partial Q/\partial L = 8L^{-.6}K^{.5}$
   (c) $MP_K = \partial Q/\partial K = 10L^{.4}K^{-.5}$
   (d) $Q = (20)30^{.4}20^{.5} = 348.65$
   (e) Total Factor Payment $= (8)(30^{-.6})(20^{.5})(30) + (10)(30^{.4})(20^{-.5})(20) = 313.79$
   $r = 0.9$, so $rQ = 0.9(348.65) = 313.79$

5. (a) $0 = 1 + x^{.5}y^{-.5}dy/dx + x^{-.5}y^{.5} + dy/dx$
   $dy/dx(x^{.5}y^{-.5} + 1) = -(1 + x^{-.5}y^{.5})$

   $$-\frac{dy}{dx} = \frac{1 + (y/x)^{.5}}{1 + (x/y)^{.5}} = \frac{\dfrac{x^{.5} + y^{.5}}{x^{.5}}}{\dfrac{y^{.5} + x^{.5}}{y^{.5}}} = \frac{y^{.5}}{x^{.5}} = MRS_{x\,for\,y}$$

   (b) $\partial U/\partial x = 1 + x^{-.5}y^{.5}$
   $\partial U/\partial y = 1 + x^{.5}y^{-.5}$
   $MRS_{x\text{ for }y} = (1 + x^{-.5}y^{.5})/(1 + x^{.5}y^{-.5}) = y^{.5}/x^{.5}$
   (c) $dU = (\partial U/\partial x)dx + (\partial U/\partial y)dy$
   $0 = (1 + x^{-.5}y^{.5})dx + (1 + x^{.5}y^{-.5})dy$
   $-dy/dx = y^{.5}/x^{.5} = MRS_{x\text{ for }y}$
   Of course, $y^{.5}/x^{.5}$ may be written $(y/x)^{.5}$.

6. (a) $$Q = \frac{10 - 2P}{P} = 10P^{-1} - 2$$
   $$dQ/dp = -10P^{-2} = -10/P^2$$
   $$\eta = -\frac{dQ}{dP}\cdot\frac{P}{Q} = \frac{10}{P^2}\cdot\frac{P}{(10 - 2P)/P} = \frac{10}{10 - 2P} = \frac{10}{10 - 2(2)} = 1.67$$

   if Q = 3, P = 2 from the original demand curve.

   (b) Solve the original equation for P, explicitly:

   $PQ = 10 - 2P$
   $PQ + 2P = 10$
   $P(Q + 2) = 10$
   $P = 10/(Q + 2)$
   Since TR = PQ, we have
   $TR = 10Q/(Q + 2)$

   $$MR = \frac{d(TR)}{dQ} = \frac{(Q + 2)(10) - 10Q(1)}{(Q + 2)^2} = .8,$$

   when Q = 3

   $MR = P(1 - 1/\eta)$
   $0.8 = 2(1 - 1/\eta)$
   $\eta = 1.67$

7. $dQ/dP = -20P^{-3}$
$\eta = -(dQ/dP)(P/Q) = 20P^{-3}(P/10P^{-2}) = 20P^{-2}/10P^{-2} = 2$

8. $\ln Q = \ln 10 - 2 \ln P$
$(1/Q)(dQ/dP) = -2(1/P)(dP/dP)$
$-(P/Q)(dQ/dP) = 2 = \eta$

9. (a) $dS/dt = (.15)20e^{.15t}$
$(dS/dt)/S = (.15)20e^{.15t}/20e^{.15t} = .15$
(b) $dS/dt = rAe^{rt}$
$(dS/dt)/S = rAe^{rt}/Ae^{rt} = r$
(c) $S = 20e^{.15(5)} = 42.34$ (thousands of pies per quarter)

10. (a) $MC = d(TC)/dq = 20e^{.2q}$
(b) $ATC = TC/q = (100e^{.2q})/q$
(c) Fixed costs are the level of costs at output of zero ($q = 0$), or
$FC = 100e^{.2(0)} = 100$ (100,000 dollars)
(d) $(100e^{.2q})/q = 20e^{.2q}$
$q = (100e^{.2q})/(20e^{.2q}) = 100/20 = 5$ (five thousand bats per month)
(e) $d(TC)/dq = bAe^{bq}$
$ATC = (Ae^{bq})/q$
$bAe^{bq} = (Ae^{bq})/q$
$q = (Ae^{bq})/(bAe^{bq}) = 1/b$

Chapter 5

1. (a) $d^2y/dx^2 = 0$
(b) $d^2y/dx^2 = 8x + 2$
(c) $d^2y/dx^2 = 72x - 12$
(d) $d^2y/dx^2 = 0$

2. (a) $dy/dx = -4x + 26 = 0, x = 6.5$
$d^2y/dx^2 = -4 < 0$, therefore a maximum
$\pi = y = -2(6.5)^2 + 26(6.5) - 60 = 24.5$
(b) $dy/dx = -3x^2 + 30x = 0, x = 0, x = 10$
$d^2y/dx^2 = -6x + 30 = -6(10) + 30 = -30$, therefore a maximum at $x = 10$
$d^2y/dx^2 = -6x + 30 = -6(0) + 30 = +30$, therefore a minimum at $x = 0$
At $x = 10$, $\pi = y = -(10)^3 + (15)10^2 - 10 = 490$
At $x = 0$, $\pi = y = -(0)^3 + (15)0^2 - 10 = -10$

3. The relative minimum at $x = 0$ for the profit function in part (b) of problem 2 means that output is zero. The negative profit could represent short-run fixed costs.

4. $dy/dx = 12x - 24 = 0, x = 2$
$d^2y/dx^2 = 12$, therefore a minimum at $x = 2$ (2 thousand balls per year)
$y = (6)2^2 - 24(2) + 50 = 26$ (dollars per ball)

5. (a) $dy/dx = 3x^2 + 2x - 1 = 0$, solutions are $x = -1$, $x = ⅓$
$d^2y/dx^2 = 6x + 2 = -4$ for $x = -1$ and $+4$ for $x = ⅓$, therefore the function is a maximum for $x = -1$ and a minimum for $x = ⅓$. For $x = 1$, $y = -5$. For $x = ⅓$, $y = -6.185$.
(b) $dy/dx = 2x^2 - 4x - 30 = 0$, solutions are $x = 5$, $x = -3$.
$d^2y/dx^2 = 4x - 4 = 16$ for $x = 5$ and -16 for $x = -3$, therefore the function is a minimum for $x = 5$ and a maximum for $x = -3$. For $x = 5$, $y = -56.67$. For $x = -3$, $y = 114$.

6. (a) $\partial z/\partial x = f_x = y + 2x - 3 = 0$
$\partial z/\partial y = f_y = 2y + x + 3 = 0$
Solving these equations, $x = 3, y = -3$.
$f_{xx} = 2, f_{yy} = 2, f_{xy} = 1$
$(f_{xx})(f_{yy}) - (f_{xy})2 = 3 > 0$
A relative minimum exists at $x = 3, y = -3, z = 1$.

(b) $\partial z/\partial x = f_x = 60 - 4x = 0$
$\partial z/\partial y = f_y = 100 - 2y = 0$
Solving these equations, $x = 15, y = 50$.
$f_{xx} = -4, f_{yy} = -2, f_{xy} = 0$
$(f_{xx})(f_{yy}) - (f_{xy})^2 = 8 > 0$
A relative minimum exists at $x = 15, y = 50, z = 3590$.

(c) $\partial z/\partial x = f_x = 2x = 0$
$\partial z/\partial y = f_y = -4y + 12 = 0$
Solving these equations, $x = 0, y = 3$.
$f_{xx} = 2, f_{yy} = -4, f_{xy} = 0$
$(f_{xx})(f_{yy}) - (f_{xy})^2 = -8 < 0$
A saddle point exists at $x = 0, y = 3, z = 18$.

(d) $\partial z/\partial x = f_x = 2x = 0$
$\partial z/\partial y = f_y = 2y - 2 = 0$
Solving these equations, $x = 0, y = 1$.
$f_{xx} = 2, f_{yy} = 2, f_{xy} = 0$
$(f_{xx})(f_{yy}) - (f_{xy})^2 = 4 > 0$
A relative minimum exists at $x = 0, y = 1, z = 0$.

7. (a) $L = x^2 + y^2 + xy - \lambda(2x - y - 7)$
$L_x = 2x + y - 2\lambda = 0$
$L_y = 2y + x + \lambda = 0$
$L_\lambda = 7 + y - 2x = 0$
From L_x and L_y, $x = -1.25y$. Substitution into L_λ yields $x = 2.5, y = -2$.
$L_{xx} = 2, L_{yy} = 2, L_{xy} = 1$
$(L_{xx})(L_{yy}) - (L_{xy})^2 = 3 > 0$
A relative minimum exists at $x = 2.5, y = -2, z = 5.25$

(b) $L = 3xy - \lambda(2x + 3y - 100)$
$L_x = 3y - 2\lambda = 0$
$L_y = 3x - 3\lambda = 0$
$L_\lambda = -2x - 3y + 100 = 0$
From L_x and L_y, $x = 1.5y$. Substitution into L_λ yields $x = 25$, $y = 16.67$.
$L_{xx} = 0$, $L_{yy} = 0$, $L_{xy} = 3$

The second-order conditions are not met. However, if other combinations of x and y that satisfy the constraint (for example, $x = 23.5$, $y = 17.67$ and $x = 26$, $y = 16$) are evaluated for the objective function, the value of U falls. Therefore, a relative maximum is indicated for $x = 25$, $y = 16.67$, $U = 1250$.

Chapter 6

1. (a) $\pi = TR - TC$
$\pi = 89q - (50 + 100q - 6q^2 + \frac{1}{3}q^3)$
$\pi = 89q - 50 - 100q + 6q^2 - \frac{1}{3}q^3$

For profit maximization:

$d\pi/dq = 89 - 100 + 12q - q^2 = 0$
$q^2 - 12q + 11 = 0$
$(q - 1)(q - 11) = 0$
$q = 1, q = 11$

Second-order condition:

$d^2\pi/dq^2 = 12 - 2q$

when $q = 1$, $d^2\pi/dq^2 = 10 > 0$, therefore profit is a minimum
when $q = 11$, $d^2\pi/dq^2 = -10 < 0$, therefore profit is a maximum

(b) $TC = 50 + 100(11) - 6(11)^2 + \frac{1}{3}(11)^3 = 867.67$
$TR = 89(11) = 979$
$\pi = 979 - 876.67 = 111.33$

(c) $\pi = 68q - 50 - 100q + 6q^2 - \frac{1}{3}q^3$

For profit maximization:

$d\pi/dq = 68 - 100 + 12q - q^2 = 0$
$q^2 - 12q + 32 = 0$
$(q - 4)(q - 8) = 0$
$q = 4, q = 8$

Second-order condition:

$d^2\pi/dq^2 = 12 - 2q$

when $q = 4$, $d^2\pi/dq^2 = 4 > 0$, therefore profit is a minimum
when $q = 8$, $d^2\pi/dq^2 = -4 < 0$, therefore profit is a maximum

(d) $TC = 50 + 100(8) - 6(8)^2 + \frac{1}{3}(8)^3 = 636.67$
$TR = 68(8) = 544$
$\pi = 544 - 636.67 = -92.67$ (loss)

(e) No, fixed costs are only \$50. The firm would lose less by shutting down in the short run.

2. (a) $10,000 = 10K + 20L$
(b) $G = K^{.5}L^{.5} - \lambda(10K + 20L - 10,000)$
(c) First-order conditions:

$G_K = .5K^{-.5}L^{.5} - \lambda 10 = 0$
$G_L = .5K^{.5}L^{-.5} - \lambda 20 = 0$
$G_\lambda = 10,000 - 10K - 20L$
$\lambda = (K^{-.5}L^{.5})/20$
$\lambda = (K^{.5}L^{-.5})/40$

Setting the last two equations equal ($\lambda = \lambda$):

$K = 2L$

Substituting into the iso-cost equation:

$10,000 = 10(2L) + 20L$
$10,000 = 40L$
$L = 250$
$K = 500$

The output level is

$Q = 500^{.5}250^{.5} = 353.55339$

The second-order conditions test fails; that is, $G_{KK}G_{LL} - (G_{KL})^2 = 0$. A good alternative is to assume you employ one more K or one more L, staying on the iso-cost line and evaluating the level of output. For example, if one more K is employed, one-half fewer L would be purchased, and output would be

$Q = 501^{.5}249.5^{.5} = 353.55268$

and to employ one more labor would require that two fewer capital be purchased:

$Q = 498^{.5}251^{.5} = 353.55056$

These cases result in less output; therefore, a maximum exists for $L = 250$ and $K = 500$.

3. (a) $G = K^{.5}L^{.5} - \lambda(rK + wL - R)$
(b) First-order conditions:

$G_K = .5K^{-.5}L^{.5} - \lambda r = 0$ (1)
$G_L = .5K^{.5}L^{-.5} - \lambda w = 0$ (2)
$G_\lambda = R - rK - wL = 0$ (3)

Now rewrite Equations 1 and 2 with K and L on the left-hand side:

$K = .5K^{.5}L^{.5}/\lambda r$ (1′)
$L = .5K^{.5}L^{.5}/\lambda w$ (2′)

Substitute Equations 1′ and 2′ into 3 to obtain

$$R - r(.5K^{.5}L^{.5}/\lambda r) - w(.5K^{.5}L^{.5}/\lambda w) = 0$$

canceling the r's and w's:

$$R - .5K^{.5}L^{.5}/\lambda - .5K^{.5}L^{.5}/\lambda = 0$$

or

$$R = K^{.5}L^{.5}/\lambda$$

and

$$\lambda = K^{.5}L^{.5}/R$$

Now substitute this expression for λ back into 1′ and 2′:

$$K = \frac{.5K^{.5}L^{.5}}{(r)K^{.5}L^{.5} / R} = .5(R/r) = R/2r$$

$$L = \frac{.5K^{.5}L^{.5}}{(w)K^{.5}L^{.5} / R} = .5(R/w) = R/2w$$

These are the input demand functions.

(c) $\pi = K^{.5}L^{.5} - rK - wL$

$$\partial\pi/\partial L = .5K^{.5}L^{-.5} - w = 0 \qquad (4)$$

$$\partial\pi/\partial K = .5K^{-.5}L^{.5} - r = 0 \qquad (5)$$

Equations 4 and 5 can be written as

$$w = .5K^{.5}L^{-.5} \qquad (4')$$

$$r = .5K^{-.5}L^{.5} \qquad (5')$$

Now substitute the right-hand sides of 4′ and 5′ into the iso-cost equation:

$$R = .5K^{.5}L^{-.5}(L) + .5K^{-.5}L^{.5}(K) = K^{.5}L^{.5}$$

then

$$L^{.5} = R/K^{.5} \qquad (6)$$

since from Equation 4 or 4′ of this problem

$$K^{.5} = 2wL^{.5}$$

we can substitute into Equation 6 to obtain

$$L^{.5} = R/2wL^{.5}$$

or

$$L = R/2w$$

Similarly,

$$K^{.5} = R/2rK^{.5}$$

or

$$K = R/2r$$

4. Since K = 10,

$$Q = 120L^2(10)^2 - L^3(10)^3 = 12000L^2 - 1000L^3$$
$$dQ/dL = 24000L - 3000L^2 = 0$$
$$24 - 3L = 0$$
$$L = 8$$

5. $\partial Q/\partial L = (30 - 2L)(100K - K^2) = 0$

This derivative is zero for any of these values: L = 15, K = 0, or K = 100. K = 0 and K = 100 are ruled out, since output would be zero (from the original production function).

$$\partial Q/\partial K = (30L - L^2)(100 - 2K) = 0$$

This derivative is zero for any of these values: L = 0, L = 30, or K = 50. As above, L = 0 and L = 30 are ruled out because output would be zero. The correct solution values are L = 15 and K = 50. Output from the production function is 562,500 labels per month, since

$$Q = (30\cdot15 - 15^2)(100\cdot50 - 50^2) = 562{,}500$$

6. The new supply function after the imposition of the tax is

$$P = Q_s + t$$

Setting demand and supply price equal,

$$120 - 3Q_d = Q_s + t$$

since $Q_d = Q_s$ in equilibrium, we can solve for t:

$$t = 120 - 4Q$$

Total tax receipts (T) equal tQ, or

$$T = 120Q - 4Q^2$$

To maximize T,

$$dT/dQ = 120 - 8Q = 0$$

or

$$Q = 15$$

and

$$t = 120 - 4(15) = 60$$

Since

$$d^2T/dQ^2 = -8$$

we know we have found a maximum for tax revenues. The level of tax revenues is 60·15 = 900 ($90,000 dollars per quarter, because Q is in hundreds).

7. (a) The demand curve may be written as

$$P = 200 - 2(q_1 + q_2)$$

where q_1 and q_2 are the individual outputs of firm 1 and firm 2, respectively. Since mc = 0, profit for firm 1 is price times q_1:

$$\pi_1 = 200q_1 - 2q_1^2 - 2q_1q_2$$

To maximize π_1, differentiate with respect to q_1 and set the derivative equal to zero:

$$d\pi_1/dq_1 = 200 - 4q_1 - 2q_2 = 0$$

Solving for q_1 yields the reaction function for firm 1:

$$q_1 = 50 - \tfrac{1}{2}q_2$$

Similarly, the reaction function for firm 2 is found to be

$$q_2 = 50 - \tfrac{1}{2}q_1$$

(b) To find the equilibrium quantity, substitute either firm's reaction function into the other's. Substituting the reaction function for firm 1 into that for firm 2 gives

$$q_2 = 50 - \tfrac{1}{2}(50 - \tfrac{1}{2}q_2) = 50 - 25 + \tfrac{1}{4}q_2$$

Solving for q_2:

$$q_2 = 33\tfrac{1}{3}$$

Similarly, the output of firm 1 can be shown to be 33⅓ as well. The market price is then

$$P = 200 - 2(66\tfrac{2}{3}) = 66\tfrac{2}{3}$$

(c) Since mc = 0, and under competition P = mc, price is zero. If P = 0, Q = 100.

For monopoly, profit is P·Q or

$$\pi = 200Q - 2Q^2$$

Differentiate this profit function with respect to Q, set the result equal to zero, and solve for Q:

$$d\pi/dQ = 200 - 4Q = 0$$
$$Q = 50,\ P = 100$$

The Cournot duopoly solution falls between monopoly and competition in terms of prices and quantities.

(d) With the addition of marginal cost, the profit function from part a for firm 1 becomes

$$\pi_1 = 200q_1 - 2q_1^2 - 2q_1q_2 - 40q_1$$

Differentiate this function, set it equal to zero, and solve for q_1 to obtain the new reaction function for firm 1:

$$d\pi_1/dq_1 = 200 - 4q_1 - 2q_2 - 40 = 0$$

and solving for q_1,

$$q_1 = 40 - \tfrac{1}{2}q_2$$

Similarly, the reaction function of firm 2 is found to be

$$q_2 = 40 - \tfrac{1}{2}q_1$$

(e) Substituting q_2 into the equation for q_1:

$$q_1 = 40 - \tfrac{1}{2}(40 - \tfrac{1}{2}q_1)$$
$$q_1 = 20 + \tfrac{1}{4}q_1$$
$$q_1 = 26\tfrac{2}{3}$$

and by a similar procedure,

$$q_2 = 26\tfrac{2}{3}$$

so market output is 53⅓ and price is

$$P = 200 - 2(q_1 + q_2) = 200 - 2(53\tfrac{1}{3}) = 93\tfrac{1}{3}$$

(f) For monopoly, profit is now total revenue minus total cost, P·Q – 40Q:

$$\pi = 200Q - 2Q^2 - 40Q$$

Differentiating and setting the result equal to zero,

$$d\pi/dQ = 200 - 4Q - 40 = 0$$
$$Q = 40, \text{ and } P = 120$$

For the competitive model P = MC, therefore P = 40. And if P = 40, Q = 80. Again, the Cournot duopoly solution fits nicely between monopoly and competitive results.

8. (a) $\pi = P_1q_1 + P_2q_2 - [24{,}000{,}000 + 8000(q_1 + q_2)]$
$\pi = (20000 - 3q_1)q_1 + (15000 - q_2)q_2 - [24{,}000{,}000 + 8000(q_1 + q_2)]$
$\pi = 20000q_1 - 3q_1^2 + 15000q_2 - q_2^2 - 24{,}000{,}000 - 8000q_1 - 8000q_2$
(b) $\partial\pi/\partial q_1 = 20000 - 6q_1 - 8000 = 0$
$q_1 = 2000$
$\partial\pi/\partial q_2 = 15000 - 2q_2 - 8000 = 0$
$q_2 = 3500$
(c) $P_1 = 20000 - 3(2000) = 14000$ (dollars)
$P_2 = 15000 - 3500 = 11500$ (dollars)
(d) $\pi = 14000(2000) + 11500(3500) - [24{,}000{,}000 + 8000(2000 + 3500)]$
$\pi = 250{,}000$
(e) $\eta_1 = -(dq_1/dp_1)\cdot(p_1/q_1) = -(-\tfrac{1}{3})(14000/2000) = 2\tfrac{1}{3}$
$\eta_2 = -(dq_2/dp_2)\cdot(p_2/q_2) = -(-1)(11500/3500) = 3.286$

Generally, under profit-maximizing price discrimination, the group with the lower coefficient of price elasticity is charged the higher price. More specifically, the exact relationship is given by the relationship between marginal revenue and price:

$$MR = P(1 - \frac{1}{\eta})$$

Since profit maximization requires MC = MR,

$$MC = P(1 - \frac{1}{\eta})$$

9. (a) $L = 10D + 80P - D^2 - 2P^2 + \lambda(38 - 1/2D - 2P)$
   (b) First-order conditions:

$$L_D = \partial L/\partial D = 10 - 2D - \tfrac{1}{2}\lambda = 0$$
$$L_P = \partial L/\partial P = 80 - 4P - 2\lambda = 0$$
$$L_\lambda = \partial L/\partial \lambda = 38 - \tfrac{1}{2}D - 2P = 0$$

Solving the first two derivatives for λ:

$$\lambda = 20 - 4D$$
$$\lambda = 40 - 2P$$

Setting λ =λ:

$$20 - 4D = 40 - 2P$$

or

$$P = 2D + 10$$

Substituting into the budget constraint:

$$38 = \tfrac{1}{2}D + 2(2D + 10)$$
$$D = 4$$

and also from the budget line, if D = 4, P = 18.

(c) Second-order conditions:

$$L_{DD} = -2$$
$$L_{PP} = -4$$
$$L_{DP} = L_{PD} = 0$$
$$(L_{DD})(L_{PP}) - (L_{DP})^2 = 8$$

Therefore, the second-order conditions for a maximum are met.

Index

Note: Locators in *italics* indicate additional charts, and *n* indicates footnote.